MEL BAY'S

OLD-TIME GOSPEL

SONGBOOK

By Wayne Erbsen

A recording of the music in this book is now available. The publisher strongly recommends the use of this recording along with the text to insure accuracy of interpretation and ease in learning.

Visit us on the Web at http://www.melbay.com — E-mail us at email@melbay.com

Step Inside

S tep inside and come on in—there's going to be a singing. Hang up your overcoat, take off your hat and make yourself comfortable. There are a few seats left right over there.

As you turn the pages of "The Old-Time Gospel Songbook" memories of old familiar hymns will come out to greet you like long lost friends. As you sing your way through the book, you'll find songs of every persuasion—songs to warm your heart, fill your soul, and even some to get your toes to tapping and your hands to clapping. Some songs will tell stories from the Bible, while others will show a glimpse of Heaven, a walk through a lonesome graveyard, a visit to an old-time church or tent revival, or a sermon by a fire-and-brimstone preacher. Most of these religious songs come from American soil, but the imagery of the poetry, and some of the twists and turns of the melodies have been borrowed from unknown songwriters in ancient times and foreign lands.

Because gospel songs have evolved from earlier forms of sacred music, we will take you on a little historical expedition to look at the roots of gospel music—shape-note hymns, religious folk songs, camp meeting spirituals, sentimental religious songs, and finally, gospel songs. As you go through the book, you'll find a few songs so old they've sprouted whiskers, and others, nearly forgotten, with a few specks of rust on them. But all the songs have been preserved in musical notation and can be polished smooth again with only a few singings.

Gospel music is best sung in groups, but you needn't wait until Sunday to sing them. The oldest trick for getting people together is to offer to feed them, so throw a pie supper, pot luck, or dinner-on-the-grounds. After the group has demolished the feast, flop open your copy of "The Old-Time Gospel Songbook" and gather everyone around for an old-fashioned singing they won't soon forget.

Photo by Walker Evans
Reproduced from the collections of the Library of Congress

Cedar Grove, North Carolina, May 1940
Photo by Jack Delano
Reproduced from the collection of the Library of Congress

Contents

Hymns

When the Pilgrims set sail for the New World, there was precious little cargo space to store their belongings. Among their treasured possessions most did bring with them their Bible and the memory of the psalms. Although they were known to have sung psalms on board the Mayflower, the task of dealing with a strange and harsh environment left little time for developing psalm-singing in America. The small handful of psalms that were known were painfully rendered in unison with no instrumentation and were sung so slowly that one singer remembered, "I myself have twice in one note paused for breath." The few worn psalters could not be shared by whole congregations, so songleaders would recite or "line-out" the words for everyone to follow.

The dreadful condition of psalm-singing did not continue forever; a spirit of revival and reform was in the air. As early as 1721 songbooks were published by Rev. John Tufts and others who added to the meager store of psalms. Singing-schools began to teach music by note instead of by rote. In 1734, John Wesley labored to bring about a revival in church singing by publishing "A Collection of Psalms and Hymns" which was the first book containing hymns to be published in the colonies. Half of the hymns in Wesley's collection were penned by Dr. Isaac Watts who was the first to break away from the cherished belief that the only acceptable religious songs were the psalms.

Once people overcame the notion that the only "true" religious music was the faithful singing of the psalms, what have been called "folk hymns" sprang up everywhere. They drew their inspiration from the words of the Bible and took familiar tunes from every available source. Proceeding on the principle "Why should the Devil have all the good tunes?" melodies for folk hymns came from sea chanteys, English ballads like *Barbara Allen*, fiddle tunes such as *Fisher's Hornpipe*, and popular sentimental songs like *Darling Nelly Gray*, and *Home Sweet Home*. These compositions were the result of the need for hymns which represented the popular taste. The lyrics were put in the plain, everyday language of the common man, and set to familiar and often lively tunes that everyone could sing.

As religious music developed in the 19th and 20th centuries, taproots began to grow from the psalms and hymns—religious folk songs, shape-note hymns, camp meeting spirituals, sentimental religious songs, and finally gospel songs. While the psalms and hymns were directed only to one of the members of The Holy Trinity, these later religious songs were addressed more to man, and spoke of his personal search for salvation.

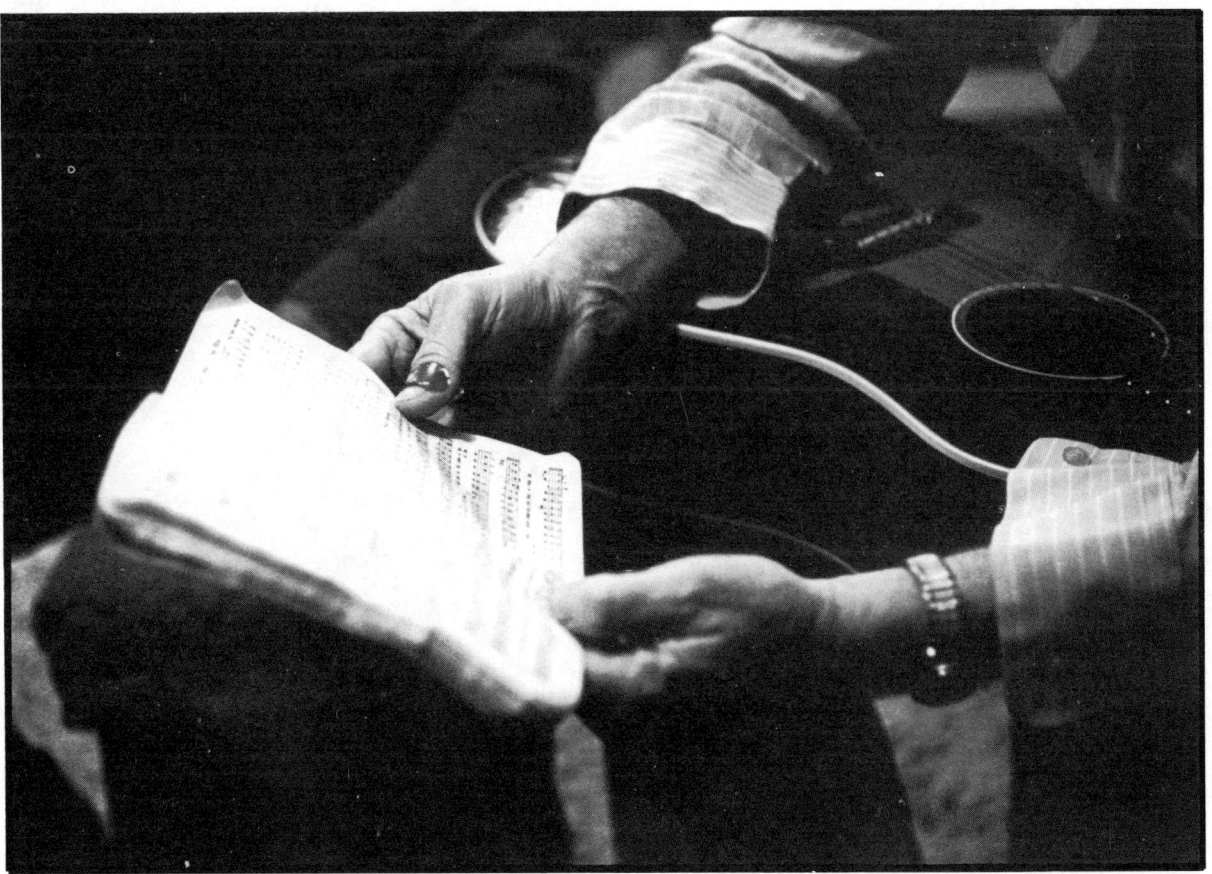

Photo by Wayne Erbsen

Religious Folk Songs

The forces that created folk songs are as old as singing itself. They started when some unknown singer unconsciously altered the text or tune of some ancient song. As long as they are dependent on man's fallible memory, songs are bound to change. Religious folk songs, like their secular cousin, are reshaped by the countless unknown voices that sing them. Each singer's natural creativity, lapses in memory, and personal experiences help to give the song a new turn. After untold such renderings, cumbersome wording and awkward phrasing are smoothed out, as singers try to adapt their songs to the context in which they are sung.

Unlike the folk hymns, which were changed to suit the demands of the harmony then being taught in the popular singing-schools, religious folk songs were not part of any organized religion. While folk hymns appeared in denominational hymn books alongside the hymns of noted composers, religious folk songs remained strictly in the oral tradition until fairly recently because they were curiously avoided by most folk song collectors. Often sung by individuals, instead of congregations, they developed their unique forms to suit the needs of melody. Many of these melodies were built on only five or six of the seven notes of the scale. This left "gaps," creating what are called "gapped scales." Such scales made possible a lonesome, haunting sound that is scarcely heard in modern music.

Many religious folk songs took the form of secular ballads, but with religious texts. Like the traditional ballad, religious ballads told a story that often droned on for upteen verses, generally told in the first person, or story form. The religious ballad also shared with the traditional ballad occasional quirks in timing, owing to the rhythmic freedom enjoyed by some solo singers.

By now, most religious folk songs have been "captured" in print for us all to learn. The process that created these songs, however, will revive every time man turns his eyes from the printed page and unconsciously changes the song he is singing.

American Folklife Center
Photo by Carl Fleischhaer

Shape-Note Hymns

By the early 1770s singing-schools were helping to breathe life into sacred music in New England. Singing-school masters stopped in a community long enough to teach the rudiments of part-singing, musical notation, and rhythm. Despite those who looked down their noses at the newfangled "singing-schools," the master usually rented a room in a tavern to hold the classes which ran for two or three weeks. Such a room could be rented cheaply because the innkeeper knew of the patronage he would enjoy after parched throats had sung for two or three hours. On the first night, the master might lug in an armload of songbooks, a chart showing the musical symbols, or a carpetbag full of his tools—a tuning fork, tablets and pencils, a baton, and maybe a handkerchief to wipe his exasperated brow.

As students sat in a semi-circle two or three rows deep with their candles flickering, the master firmly lead the class through the fundamentals of music. They soon learned to sing in three parts while keeping the beat with an up and down motion of the right hand. When the class had reached a reasonable level of proficiency, a demonstration was held for the entire community to witness. The singing-school master then climbed back on his mule and headed down the road in search of another group of willing students.

As the country became more settled, the Yankee singing-school masters found that the bustling cities of the North had little time for such things as "singing-schools." Worse than that, many churches were importing huge organs which tended to overshadow the hymn singers with their great volume and musical complexity. All that remained for the singers was to dutifully follow the lead of the organ. Contemptuously referred to such organs as "the Devil's bagpipe," the masters reluctantly turned their mules toward the unspoiled lands to the South and West. In these areas, singing-schools became a deeply rooted part of life, and news of the coming of a singing-school master was greeted with great enthusiasm.

In an effort to simplify the teaching of singing, in the early 1800s the masters began using what have been called "shape-notes." The idea was to give each fa, so, la, or mi of the scale a characteristic shape. Once singers learned to recognize the shapes and associate them with their relative pitch on the scale, whole groups could be led through complicated hymns in short order. Legions of singers flocked to popular singing-schools to learn the shapes despite the jests of critics who called the new shapes "buckwheat notes," "patent notes," or "three-cornered sounds." Such criticism only instilled in shape-note singers a deeper determination to hold on to the shape-notes despite all adversity. They defiantly named such critics "Round Heads," after the round notes they used.

In 1846, Jesse B. Aiden published the "Christian Minstrel" which made use of seven shapes, instead of the four used in earlier methods. It became so widely used that it went through at least 171 editions and set the standard that later shape-note songbooks followed. A visit to many a country home in the South even now would reveal a small stack of worn shape-note songbooks piled neatly on the family piano. These songbooks are not only treasured relics of past times, but also vibrant testimony to the continued strength of shape-note singing today.

Quay Smathers, Swannanoa, North Carolina
Photo by David Holt

7

Camp Meeting Spirituals

In July of 1800 the first camp meeting was held on Gasper River in Logan County, Kentucky. For several days, crowds gathered for what became the start of an era of revivalistic camp meetings They came from far away on horseback, covered wagons and buckboards, and from nearby on foot. Many erected tents and makeshift lean-tos while others slept under the stars.

Kentucky offered an ideal setting for the first camp meetings. Summer roads were dry and passable, and skies were clear and warm. Many families came from long distances because their settlements did not have the luxury of a church or a full-time preacher. Here they would get to share in the excitement of hearing perhaps a dozen or more preachers from far-away North Carolina or Tennessee.

The people who came to the camp meetings were a mixture as diverse as any in America. There were the pious and the saved, as well as the scoffers and the backsliders. They came from family farms and from the outlying towns and villages. In the evening, they gathered close to improvised platforms lit by pine-knot torches and candles to hear the preaching, witness the fever of conversion, and to sing of heaven.

Since the people came from all denominations, there was no shared body of religious song that all could sing. The shortage of hymn books and the flickering light of the torches and campfires made singing the old hymns difficult even for those who knew how to read. Nor would lining-out or "deaconing" the hymns work amidst the noise of the assembled throng. What did develop has been called the "camp meeting spiritual" or "camp meeting chorus." It was discovered that if a song could be made simple and repetitive enough, large camp meeting crowds could join together in song. Familiar lines were borrowed from old hymns or from passages in the Bible and made into singable choruses or refrains that were easy to remember. Repetition rendered the spirituals so simple that it was difficult to resist the temptation to sing.

The emotionalism of these camp meeting spirituals were a welcome contrast to the sober and staid hymns remembered from church. They were often spontaneously started by one of the preachers and exuberantly taken up by the crowd. These rousing spirituals were in fact folk songs that were reshaped by the thousands of voices that sang them. The settlers who came to the camp meetings were a mixture of rich and poor, black and white, so the camp meeting spirituals were a true blending of American religious music. As such, they represent an important departure from the hymnody of the past. Religious songs now came not from the pen of a few gifted composers but from the people themselves.

Akers Tent Revival, Galax, Virginia
American Folklife Center
Photo by Terry Eiler

Sentimental Religious Songs

Americans have always had a soft spot for sentimental songs. As early as the Revolution, tearful songs of parting lovers, orphans, dying soldiers and dear old mother have remained close to the hearts of the American people. By the 1890s sentimental songs had become big business to Tin Pan Alley songwriters and publishers. Department stores opened sheet music counters and even newspapers issued supplements of the current favorites.

The popularity of sentimental songs did not go unnoticed by the composers of America's religious music. Like their secular counterparts, many were struggling to stay afloat. Some reasoned that if the people wanted sentimental songs, they would give them sentimental songs, but religious ones. These writers borrowed popular themes of mother and home for their own compositions. At the same time, Tin Pan Alley writers like Charles K. Harris were composing songs such as *Hello Central, Give Me Heaven* to cash in on themes which combined both religion and sentimentality. Although serious composers of sacred music looked down upon such efforts to capitalize on religion or to popularize sacred music, the buying public didn't seem to mind.

Interior of a church in Mississippi, June 1937
Photo by Dorothea Lange
Reproduced from the collections of the Library of Congress

Gospel Songs

Ever since the revival known as "The Great Awakening" in the middle 18th century, religious leaders have realized the importance of developing a body of song that would inspire the hearts of men and fan the flames of revival. In 1871, evangelist Dwight Moody teamed up with songleader and composer Ira Sankey and barnstormed their way first across England and then through the northern cities in America. In the wake of these revival meetings came a series of volumes known as "Gospel Hymns." The term "gospel" had been applied to sacred music as early as the 17th century. But "Gospel Hymns" now designated a kind of emotional and personal religious song that spread rapidly through northern revivals. They drew their inspiration from a long history of religious songs dating back to the early days of the colonies. Some were the standard hymns from days past and others borrowed the verse and chorus patterns from camp meeting spirituals. Others were taken from Sunday school songsters and from YMCA hymn books. Many of the songs in "Gospel Hymns" came from the recent compositions of northern songwriters. In an effort to stir the crowds that came to the revivals, the songs were written in the popular and often sentimental style of the day. Their message was strongly emotional and spoke of personal salvation and heaven. The success of this approach must be measured in terms of the estimated 50-70 million copies of "Gospel Hymns" that were sold.

Although the religious music of the South developed its own character, it was similar enough to the "Gospel Hymns" of the Northern revivals that it adopted the name "gospel." Southern gospel music evolved out of its strong tradition of religious music. Like the "Gospel Hymn," it borrowed the verse and chorus pattern from the camp meeting spiritual but combined it with the harmonies learned in Southern singing-schools and shape-note books. After the 1850s, songwriters started to compose songs to appeal to the thousands who attended shape-note singing conventions throughout the South. In order to keep singers interested in all four harmony parts, songwriters composed pieces which would challenge those raised in the shape-note tradition. The resulting gospel songs contained often complex moving parts with emotional and personal texts set to melodies in the popular style of the day.

These gospel songs particularly appealed to members of the Holiness church which was gaining prominence in the rural South after the Civil War. These conservative Christians provided solid support for gospel music at a time when the more progressive urban churches were attacking gospel music as unfit to survive the cheap wood-pulp on which they are printed.

In spite of such criticism, gospel music developed a strong and loyal following. Publishing houses such as James D. Vaughn and Stamps-Baxter furnished shape-note songbooks to the growing number of singing conventions held in rural churches in the South. These and other publishing companies developed unique merchandising techniques to sell their songbooks and promote gospel music. By 1910 James D. Vaughn organized his first gospel quartet which began touring the country selling songbooks. By the middle 1920s Vaughn had sixteen such gospel troupes on the road selling an estimated half million books a year. In 1922, Vaughn started his own record label to tap into an even larger audience.

Publishers like James D. Vaughn and Stamps-Baxter relied heavily on their touring quartets to spread gospel music to all corners of the country. Stamps-Baxter, in fact, hired only singers to work in their publishing house. By day they helped to produce paperback songbooks, and by night and on weekends their quartets sang in churches and singing conventions. Gradually, many of the quartets began to break away from the publishers and established professional careers on their own. Utilizing the techniques of secular music, radio, TV, records, and personal appearances, they have succeeded in establishing gospel music as a viable and respected form of popular music. Its style now closely parallels trends in modern country and popular music. Gospel music has come a long way since the old Yankee singing-school master braved the wilderness on muleback to teach the isolated settlers their do-re-mi's.

An itinerant preacher's automobile in town on court day.
Campton, Kentucky, September 1940
Photo by Marion Post Wolcott
Reproduced from the collections of the Library of Congress

A Beautiful Life

A *Beautiful Life* is an old-style gospel quartet that reminds us of days when the leader would "line out" verses for the congregation to follow. In this song, the lead and bass singers take turns lining out the song. On the verses, the lead sings the first phrase and the harmony echoes him. At the beginning of the chorus, ("Life's evening sun . . . ") the bass takes the lead with the harmony following him. About halfway through the chorus ("To meet the deeds . . . ") the lead singer again takes over and leads the song to the end of the chorus.

Traditional

2. To be a child of God each day
   My light must shine along the way.
   I'll sing his praise while ages roll
   And strive to help some troubled soul. *(Chorus)*

3. The only life that will endure
   Is one that's kind and good and pure.
   And so for God I'll take my stand
   Each day I'll lend a helping hand. *(Chorus)*

4. I'll help someone in time of need
   And journey on with rapid speed.
   I'll help the sick, the poor and weak
   And words of kindness to them speak. *(Chorus)*

5. While going down life's weary road
   I'll try to lift some traveler's load.
   I'll try to turn the night to day
   Make flowers bloom along the way. *(Chorus)*

Amazing Grace

It would be hard to imagine a background more unusual than that of John Newton, the composer of *Amazing Grace*. Born in 1725, he went to sea at the age of nine, after the death of his mother. He later deserted from the British navy but was caught and put in irons and whipped. He then signed on with a slave ship which carried its human cargo from Africa to America.

When Newton was twenty-three, his ship was battered by a violent storm. Thinking the vessel would go down, he prayed for the first time since his mother died. When the storm had passed he turned to God and began studying the Scriptures. He eventually became captain of a slave ship, but continued studying the Bible. After some years, he finally gave up the sea and, at the age of thirty-nine, was ordained as minister of the Church of England. Legends tell that even as the pastor of the church in Olney, England, he continued to wear the uniform of a sea captain while toting a cane in one hand and a Bible in the other.

Composing *Amazing Grace* in Olney, Newton set the words to an anonymous hymn tune. It often appears in old hymn books under the title *New Britain* or *Harmony Grove.* It later became popular at camp meeting revivals where singable choruses were often composed so the large crowds could join in the singing of this venerable old hymn.

John Newton   **Anonymous folk tune**

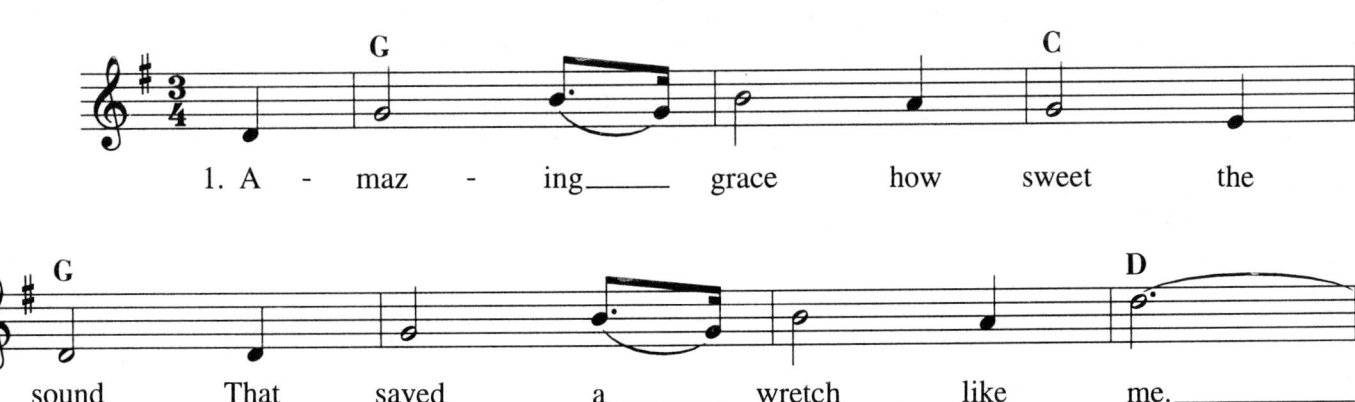

2. 'Twas grace that taught my heart to fear
   And grace my fears relieved,
   How precious did that grace appear
   The hour I first believed.

3. Through many dangers, toils and snares
   I have already come,
   'Twas grace that brought me safe thus far
   And grace will lead me home.

4. When we've been there ten thousand years
   Bright shining as the sun,
   We've no less days to sing God's praise
   Than when we first begun.

The Lemuel Smith family saying Grace before the afternoon meal, Carroll County, Virginia, April 1941
Photo by Jack Delano
Reproduced from the collections of the Library of Congress

Angel Band

O riginally entitled *My Latest Sun is Sinking Fast, Angel Band* was composed by William Bradbury and Jefferson Haskell and first appeared in J. D. Dadmun's "Melodian" (1860). Born in York, Maine, on October 6, 1816, Bradbury became an organist, piano teacher, and singing-school master as well as a prolific composer and compiler of sacred books. His fifty-nine books were said to have sold a total of over two million copies.

Jefferson Hascall   **William Batchelder Bradbury**

1. My lat - est sun is sink - ing fast, My race is near - ly run.___

My strong - est tri - als now__ are past, My__ tri - umph is be - gun. _____

Chorus

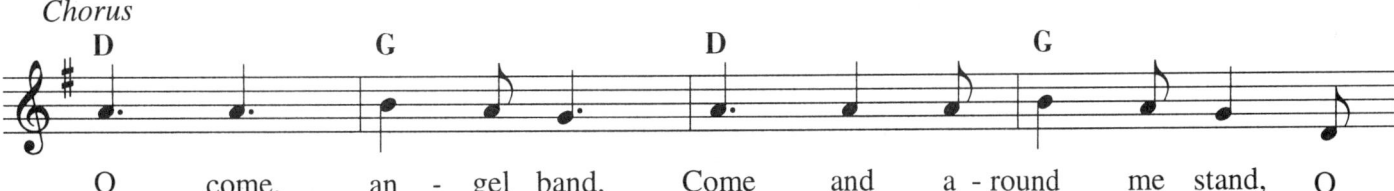

O come, an - gel band, Come and a - round me stand, O

bear me a - way on your snow - y wings, To my im - mor - tal home,___ O

bear me a - way on your snow - y wings, To my im - mor - tal home.___

2. I know I'm nearing the holy ranks
   Of friends and kindred dear,
   For I brushed the dews on Jordan's banks
   The crossing must be near. *(Chorus)*

3. I've almost gained my heavenly home
   My spirit loudly sings,
   The holy one, behold they come!
   I hear the noise of wings! *(Chorus)*

4. O bear my longing heart to Him
   Who bled and died for me,
   Whose blood now cleanses from all sin
   And gives me victory. *(Chorus)*

Angel Band

(Bluegrass Version)

Jefferson Hascall   William Batchelder Bradbury

My lat - est sun ___ is sink - ing fast, My
My strong - est tri - als now ___ are past, My

race is near - ly run. _____ Oh come, _____
tri - umph is be - gun. _____

an - gel band, Come and _____ a - round me stand, Oh

bear me a - way on your snow - y wings, To my im -

mor - tal home, _____ Oh bear me a - way on your

snow - y wings, To my im - mor - tal ___ home. _____

2. O bear my longing heart to Him
   Who bled and died for me,
   Whose blood now cleanses from all sin
   And gives me victory. *(Chorus)*

3. I've almost gained my heavenly home
   My spirit loudly sings,
   The holy ones, behold they come!
   I hear the noise of wings! *(Chorus)*

Are You Washed in the Blood?

Born on May 7, 1839 in Orwigsburg, Pennsylvania, Elisha A. Hoffman spent most of the next ninety years serving God as minister of the Evangelical United Brethren Church. A prolific writer of gospel songs, Hoffman included many of his compositions, and those of his wife, in "Happy Songs for Sunday School" (1876) and "Sunday School Songs" (1880). In 1888 he set the music to Rev. Anthony J. Showalter's poem *Leaning on the Everlasting Arms.* His *Are You Washed in the Blood?* was first copyrighted in 1879.

Rev. E. A. Hoffman   Rev. E. A. Hoffman

1. Have you been to Je - sus for the clean - sing power? Are you

washed in the blood of the Lamb?   Are you ful - ly trust-ing in His grace this hour? Are you
Are your gar-ments spot-less? Are they white as snow? Are you

washed   in   the   blood   of   the   Lamb?   Are you   washed (are you washed) in   the
washed   in   the   blood   of   the   Lamb?

blood,   (in   the   blood)   In   the   soul - clean - sing   blood   of   the   Lamb?

2. Are you walking daily by the Savior's side?
   Are you washed in the blood of the Lamb?
   Do you rest each moment in the Crucified?
   Are you washed in the blood of the Lamb? *(Chorus)*

3. When the Bridegroom cometh will your robes be white?
   Are you washed in the blood of the Lamb?
   Will your soul be ready for the mansion bright?
   Are you washed in the blood of the Lamb? *(Chorus)*

4. Lay aside the garments that are stained with sin
   And be washed in the blood of the Lamb,
   There's a fountain flowing for the soul unclean
   Oh, be washed in the blood of the Lamb. *(Chorus)*

As I Went Down in the Valley to Pray

As I Went Down in the Valley to Pray is a very old unaccompanied spiritual that has been collected from both white and black sources. It was included under the title *The Good Old Way* in "Slave Songs of the United States" (1867). The chorus belongs to a family of songs in which only one word (father, mother, sister, brother) changes each time around.

As I went down in the val-ley to pray, Stu-dy-ing a-bout that good old way. And who shall wear the star-ry crown, Good Lord, show me the way. Oh bro-thers, let's go down Come on down, Don't you want to go down,_____ Oh bro-ther, let's go down,_____ Down in the val-ley to pray.

Zion Hill Primitive Baptist Church, Surry County, North Carolina
American Folklife Center
Photo of old pew outside

The Church in the Wildwood

*T*he Church in the Wildwood can claim the distinction of being the only song known to have inspired the building of a church. It was in 1855 that the Congregational Church was organized in the village of Bradford, Iowa. Unable to afford a church of their own, the congregation met in a store, an abandoned school house, and even a lawyer's office.

William Savage Pitt, a twenty-seven year old medical student had traveled to Bradford by stagecoach. After hearing of the congregation without a church, Pitt walked to a hilltop near the town, and looked down on the Cedar River Valley. He turned to his comrades and pointed to a spot in a grove of trees where he could envision a church. Because he knew the congregation had little money, he decided it should be painted brown, as brown paint could be purchased cheaply. He named his imaginary church the little brown church in the vale.

Not long after returning home to McGregor, Iowa, Pitt composed the words and music to *The Church in the Wildwood*. Hearing of Pitt's dream of the little brown church in the vale, the new minister of Bradford's Congregational Church, Rev. John K. Nutting, encouraged his congregation to construct the church using volunteer labor and money donated from friends in the East. It was completed and dedicated on December 24, 1864. *The Church in the Wildwood* became famous as the song that inspired the building of this church.

William S. Pitts   **William S. Pitts**

There's a church in the val - ley by the wild - wood, No

love - li - er spot in the dale, No ____ place is so dear to my
No ____ spot is so dear to my

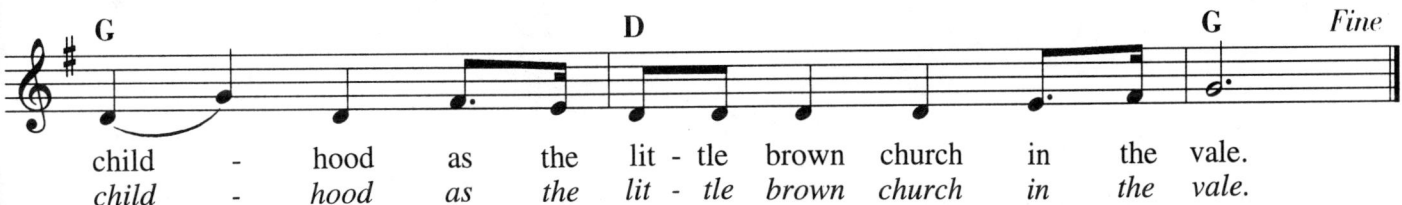

child - hood as the lit - tle brown church in the vale.
child - hood as the lit - tle brown church in the vale.

D.S. 𝄋 al Fine

Chorus

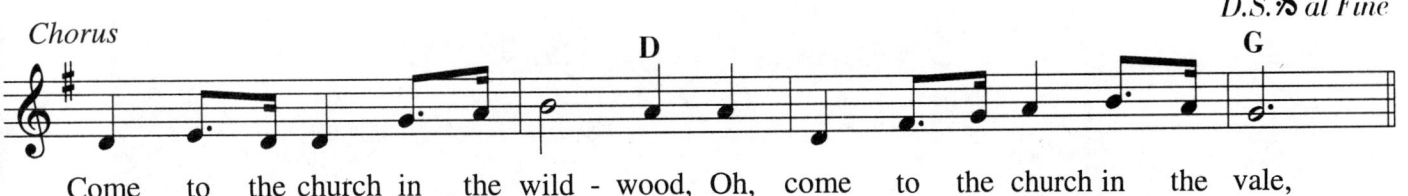

Come to the church in the wild - wood, Oh, come to the church in the vale,

2. Oh, come to the church in the wildwood
   To the trees where the wild flowers bloom,
   Where the parting hymn will be chanted
   We will weep by the side of the tomb. *(Chorus)*

3. How sweet on a clear Sabbath morning
   To list to the clear ringing bell,
   Its tones so sweetly are calling
   Oh, come to the church in the vale. *(Chorus)*

4. From the church in the valley by the wildwood
   When day fades away into night,
   I would fain from this spot of my childhood
   Wing my way to the mansions of light. *(Chorus)*

American Folklife Center
Photo by Carl Fleischhaer

Garden Creek Baptist Church, Alleghany/Wilkes County Line, North Carolina
American Folklife Center
Photo by Blanton Owen

Death is Only a Dream

Death is Only a Dream was composed by C. W. Ray and A. J. Buchanan but was copyrighted by R. M. McIntosh in 1892. It was recorded in 1934 on Victor by the Jenkins family, who were among the first family groups to record in country music. The leader of the group, Rev. Andrew Jenkins, from Jenkinsville, Georgia, was a blind Holiness preacher, musician, occasional newsboy, and important composer. His compositions numbered over 800 and included *God Put a Rainbow in the Clouds, Dream of the Miner's Child, Ben Dewberry's Final Run,* and *The Death of Floyd Collins.*

C. W. Ray

A. J. Buchanan

1. Sad - ly we sing, and with trem - u - lous breath, As we stand by the my - sti - cal stream,___ In the val - ley and by the dark riv - er of death And yet 'tis no more than a dream.

Chorus

On - ly a dream, on - ly a dream, And glo - ry be - yond the dark stream,___ How peace-ful the slum- ber, How hap - py the wak-ing for death _ is on - ly a dream.

2. Why should we weep when the weary ones rest
In the bosom of Jesus supreme,
In the mansions of glory prepared for the blest?
For death is no more than a dream. *(Chorus)*

3. Naught in the river the saints should appall
Though it frightfully dismal may seem,
In the arms of their Savior no ills can befall
They find it no more than a dream. *(Chorus)*

4. Over the turbid and onrushing tide
Doth the light of eternity gleam,
And the ransomed the darkness and storm shall outride
To wake with glad smiles from their dream. *(Chorus)*

Deep Settled Peace

Deep Settled Peace, a scarcely-heard classic of gospel music, was composed in 1928 by Kate Peters Sturgill. One of thirteen children, Kate grew up in a coal mining community near Norton, Virginia. By the age of seven, she learned the parlor organ and in her teens her brothers formed a string band and gave her a guitar, which she soon mastered. A distant relative of A. P. Carter of the famous Carter family, she often accompanied A. P. on song collecting trips. While A. P. copied down the words, Kate memorized the melody.

In the late twenties, Kate joined a group of her neighbors and formed "The Lonesome Pine Trailers." She later teamed up with Meadie Moles as "The Cumberland Valley Girls." From 1947 until 1954 they performed over radio WNV in Norton, Virginia, and at local Holiness churches and revivals.

Always an active composer of sentimental and religious songs, Kate was moved to write *Deep Settled Peace* while sitting at her father's bedside just before he died.

Kate Sturgill Peters   Kate Sturgill Peters

1. I found no rest for my soul Till I heard _____ the sto-ry told, Now I'm in _____ the Shep-herd's fold _____ And have that deep set-tled peace in my soul.

Chorus There's a deep set-tled peace in my soul, _____ I've been re-deemed and made whole, I've been washed in the blood of the Lamb And I know I un-der-stand, That deep set-tled peace in my soul. _____

2. Let not your heart be troubled so,
   If to Jesus you will go
   And of Him you'll learn to know,
   You'll have that deep settled peace in your soul. *(Chorus)*

3. Then when death around you lies,
   And you must cross the Great Divide,
   If you have Jesus on your side,
   There'll be a deep settled peace in your soul. *(Chorus)*

22

Don't You Hear Jerusalem Moan?

D*on't You Hear Jerusalem Moan?* is an old gospel/novelty song that manages to poke fun at several of the major denominations. As if the words weren't enough to make this song outrageous, the chorus has a few extra beats added for good measure. This version comes to us from the inimitable Skillet Lickers.

Well, the Meth - od - ist preach-er, you can tell him where he go; Don't you hear Je - ru - sa-lem moan? Don't_ nev-er let a chick-en get big e-nough to crow; Don't you hear Je - ru - sa - lem moan? Don't you hear Je - ru - sa - lem moan? Don't you hear Je - ru - sa - lem moan? Thank God there's a Heav-en been a-ring-ing in my soul, And my soul's got free, __ Don't you hear Je - ru - sa -a - lem __ moan?_____

2. Well, the Baptist preacher you can tell him by his coat;
   Don't you hear Jerusalem moan?
   Has a bottle in his pocket and he can hardly tote;
   Don't you hear Jerusalem moan? *(Chorus)*

3. Well, the Holy Roller preacher sure am a sight;
   Don't you hear Jerusalem moan?
   Well, he gets 'em all a-rolling and he kicks out the light;
   Don't you hear Jerusalem moan? *(Chorus)*

4. Well, the Presbyterian preacher he lives in town;
   Don't you hear Jerusalem moan?
   Neck's so stiff he can hardly look around;
   Don't you hear Jerusalem moan? *(Chorus)*

Drifting Too Far From the Shore

Charles E. Moody, the composer of *Drifting Too Far From the Shore,* had a career unlike any other gospel songwriter. His credentials for writing gospel music were indeed sound. Growing up in North Georgia, his family sang gospel songs and, in 1916, he underwent intensive study at singing-schools in Asheville, North Carolina. His musical energies, however, were directed mainly toward his band, The Georgia Yellow Hammers. This North Georgia string band recorded everything from hymns of the Sacred Harp to songs like *Pass Around the Bottle and We'll All Take a Drink.* Despite this unlikely setting, Moody's sacred compositions like *Drifting Too Far From the Shore* and *Kneel at the Cross* have become among the most popular gospel songs of the 20th century.

Charles E. Moody   Charles E. Moody

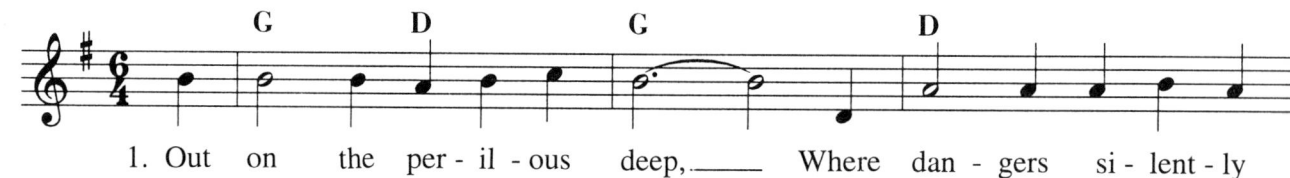

1. Out on the per - il - ous deep, Where dan - gers si - lent - ly

creep, And storms so vio - lent - ly sweep, You are

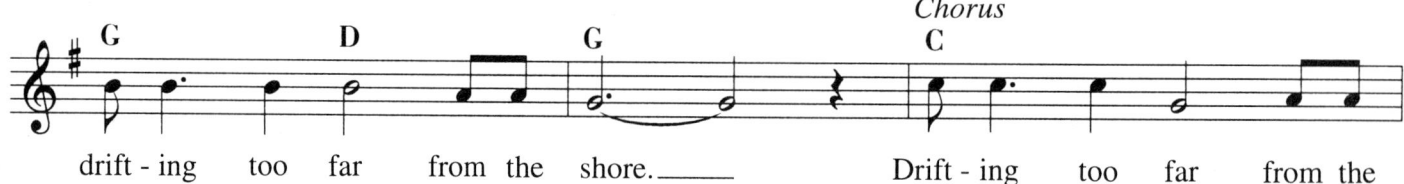

Chorus

drift - ing too far from the shore. Drift - ing too far from the

(from the shore)   (peace - ful shore)

shore, You are drift - ing too far from the shore, Come to

Je - sus to - day, Let him show you the way, You are drift-ing too far from the shore.

2. Today the tempest rolls high,
   And clouds overshadow the sky,
   Sure death is hovering nigh,
   You are drifting too far from the shore. *(Chorus)*

3. Why meet a terrible fate,
   Mercies abundantly wait,
   Turn back before it's too late,
   You are drifting too far from the shore. *(Chorus)*

Give Me the Roses Now

Give Me the Roses Now, credited to R. H. Cornelius and James Rowe, is a lovely gospel song as recorded by Jimmy Martin and Roy Lee Centers, who sang lead with Ralph Stanley. Its striking melody and poignant words make it a classic of bluegrass gospel singing.

**R. H. Cornelius
and James Rowe**

1. Won - der - ful things of folks are said When they have passed a - way; _____ Ros - es a - dorn the nar - row bed O - ver the sleep - ing clay. _____ Give me the ros - es while I ___ live Try - ing to cheer ___ me on. _____ Use - less the flow - ers that you give Af - ter the soul is gone. _____

2. Praises are heard not by the dead,
   Roses they cannot see;
   Let us not wait till souls have fled,
   Generous friends to be. *(Chorus)*

3. Faults are forgiven when folks lie
   Cold in the narrow bed;
   Let us forgive them ere they die,
   Now should the words be said. *(Chorus)*

The Glory-Land Way

James S. Torbett, the composer of the words and music to *The Glory-Land Way,* was born in Gadsden, Alabama in 1868. Trained at A. J. Showalter's Southern Normal Music Institute, Torbett worked as a singing-school teacher for some thirty-five years. *The Glory-Land Way,* his most popular composition, has become a favorite in bluegrass gospel as performed by Bill Monroe, and has become a standard in commercial gospel music as sung by the Chuck Wagon Gang, who recorded it in 1966.

J. S. Torbett   J. S. Torbett

2. List to the call, the gospel call today,
   Get in the glory-land way,
   Wanderers, come home, O hasten to obey,
   For I'm in the glo-ry-land way. *(Chorus)*

3. Onward I go, rejoicing in His love,
   I'm in the glory-land way,
   Soon I shall see Him in that home above,
   Oh, I'm in the glo-ry-land way. *(Chorus)*

The Hallelujah Side

Few gospel songwriters have enjoyed the success of the Rev. Johnson Oatman, Jr. Born on April 21, 1856 near Medford, New Jersey, he became an ordained minister, but chose not to have his own congregation. Instead, he joined his father's business and then managed an insurance agency in Mt. Holly, New Jersey. Apparently, his main energies were directed toward writing gospel songs. His many popular compositions included *The Hallelujah Side, Hand in Hand With Jesus, Higher Ground, Count Your Blessings,* and *No, Not Me.* The melody of *The Hallelujah Side* was written in 1898 by J. Howard Entwisle who later contributed the music to "Keep on the Sunny Side of Life."

Rev. Johnson Oatman, Jr.   J. Howard Entwisle

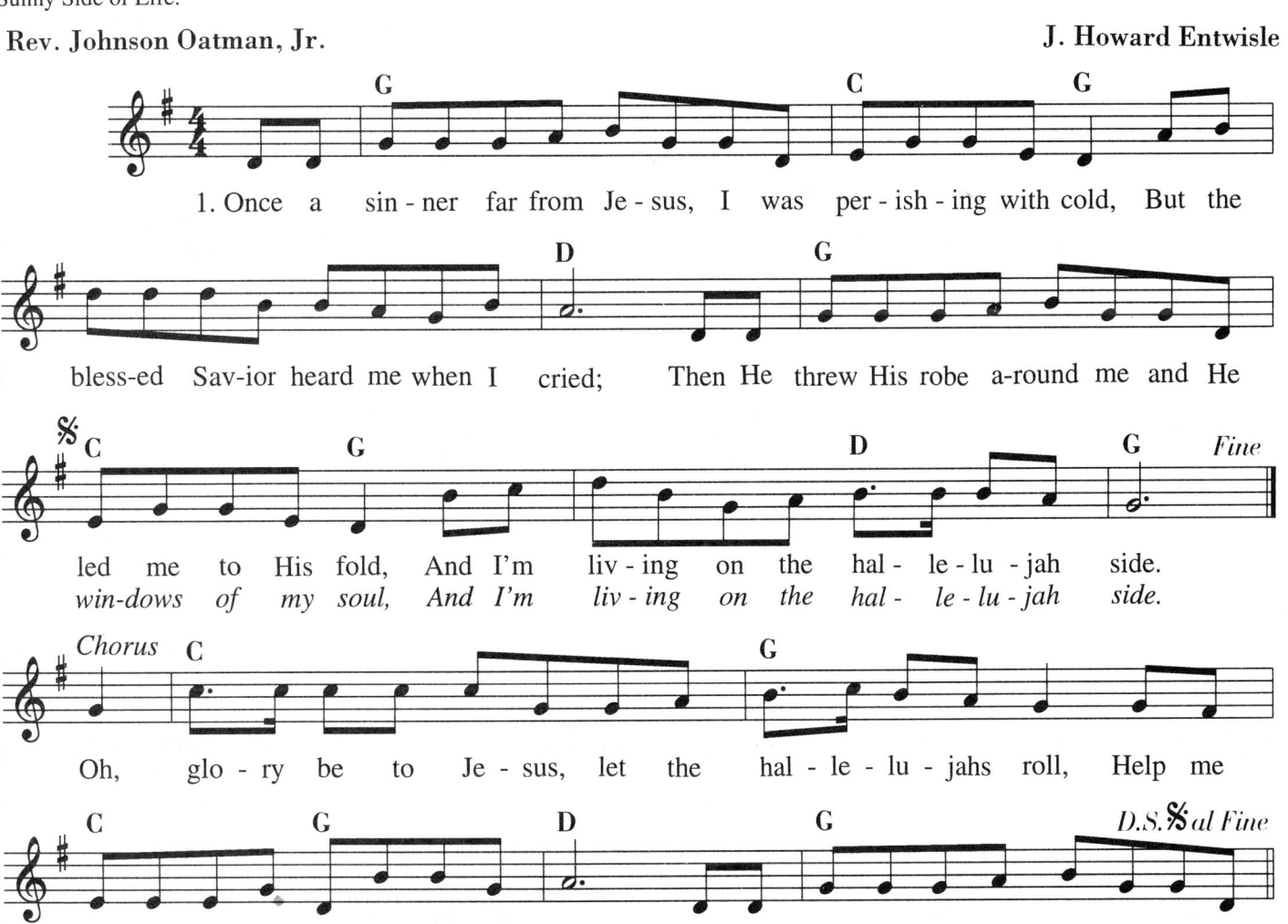

1. Once a sin-ner far from Je-sus, I was per-ish-ing with cold, But the bless-ed Sav-ior heard me when I cried; Then He threw His robe a-round me and He led me to His fold, And I'm liv-ing on the hal-le-lu-jah side.
win-dows of my soul, And I'm liv-ing on the hal-le-lu-jah side.

Chorus
Oh, glo-ry be to Je-sus, let the hal-le-lu-jahs roll, Help me ring the Sav-ior's prais-es far and wide, For I've op-ened up toward heav-en all the

2. Though the world may sweep around me with her dazzle and her dreams,
   Yet I envy not her vanities and pride,
   For my soul looks up to heaven, where the golden sunlight gleams,
   And I'm living on the hallelujah side. *(Chorus)*

3. Not for all earth's golden millions would I leave this precious place,
   Though the tempter to persuade me oft has tried,
   For I'm safe in God's pavilion, happy in His love and grace,
   And I'm living on the hallelujah side. *(Chorus)*

4. Here the sun is always shining, here the sky is always bright,
   'Tis no place for gloomy Christians to abide,
   For my soul is filled with music and my heart with great delight,
   And I'm living on the hallelujah side. *(Chorus)*

5. And upon the streets of glory, when we reach the other shore,
   And have safely crossed the Jordan's rolling tide,
   You will find me shouting "Glory" just outside my mansion door,
   Where I'm living on the hallelujah side. *(Chorus)*

Hallelujah, We Shall Rise

Hallelujah, We Shall Rise is an old-time shout song that has been popular since it was first composed by John E. Thomas and copyrighted in 1904. Born in Calhoun County, Arkansas, on December 6, 1860, Thomas studied music with T. E. Bridges and went on to help form the Trio Music Company and the Quartet Music Company of Fort Worth, Texas. Hallelujah, We Shall Rise was first popularized in early country music by Cranford and Thompson, who worked with the Red Fox Chasers, from North Carolina. It was later recorded by bluegrass bands such as The Sauceman Brothers and also the Stanley Brothers.

To show how quickly gospel songs can become folk songs, it is interesting to note that in August of 1940, folklorist Vance Randolph collected We Shall Rise, Hallelujah. The words to this "folk song" had changed almost completely from the original, with only a few words of the chorus remaining in common.

J. E. Thomas   J. E. Thomas

2. In the resurrection morning,
   What a meeting it will be,
   We shall rise (hallelujah!) we shall rise,
   When our fathers and our mothers
   And our loved ones we shall see,
   We shall rise (hallelujah!) we shall rise. (Chorus)

3. In the resurrection morning,
   Blessed thought it is to me,
   We shall rise (hallelujah!) we shall rise,
   I shall see my blessed Savior,
   Who so freely died for me,
   We shall rise (hallelujah!) we shall rise. (Chorus)

Hand in Hand With Jesus

Leonard D. Huffstutler, composer of the melody to *Hand in Hand With Jesus* can be counted among those who were the most active in promoting gospel music. Born in Alabama on June 17, 1887 and raised on a farm in Texas, Huffstutler studied gospel music with men like R. H. Cornelius, Homer Rodeheaver, and A. B. Sebren. For the next sixty years he performed with gospel quartets and taught singing-schools for Stamps-Baxter and Hartford Music. Many of his compositions like *Hand in Hand With Jesus, Deep Down in My Soul,* and *Let Us Now Praise Him* have become standards of Southern white gospel music.

Rev. Johnson Oatman, Jr.   **L. D. Huffstutler**

1. Once from my poor sin - sick soul, Christ did ev - 'ry bur - den roll,

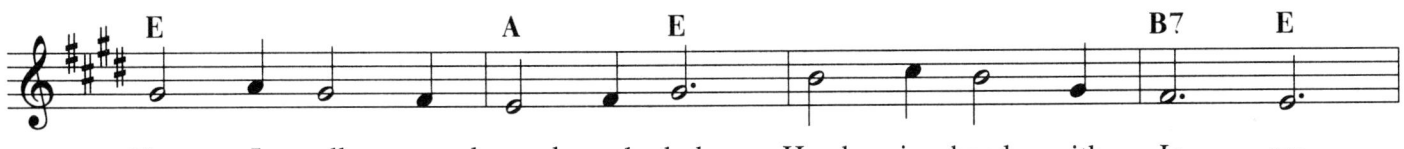

Now I walk re - deemed and whole, Hand in hand with Je - sus.

Chorus

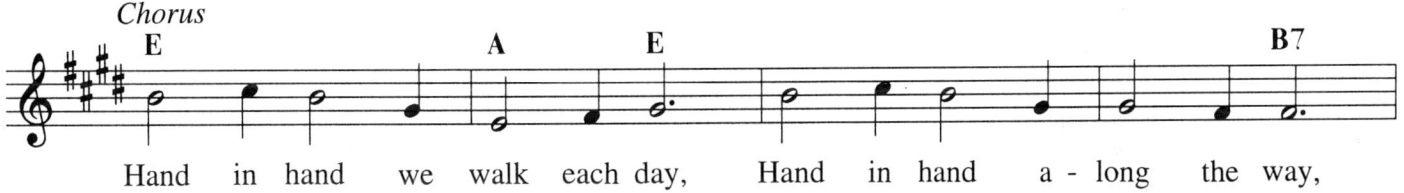

Hand in hand we walk each day, Hand in hand a - long the way,

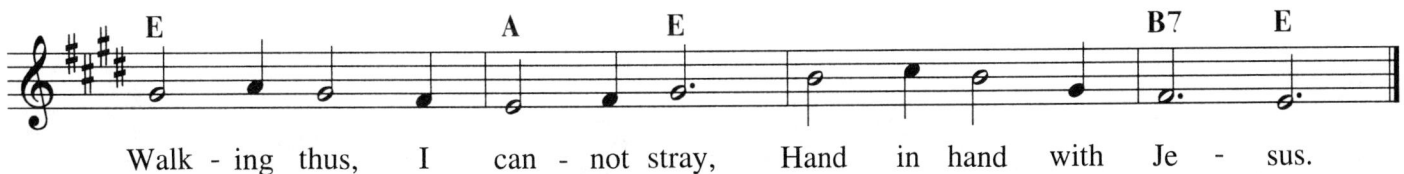

Walk - ing thus, I can - not stray, Hand in hand with Je - sus.

2. In my night of dark despair,
   Jesus heard and answered prayer,
   Now I'm walking free as air,
   Hand in hand with Jesus. *(Chorus)*

3. From the straight and narrow way,
   Praise the Lord, I cannot stray,
   For I'm walking every day,
   Hand in hand with Jesus. *(Chorus)*

He Will Set Your Fields on Fire

The words to *He Will Set Your Fields on Fire* were written by H. M. Ballew and the melody was composed by Mrs. L. L. Brackett. Still sung in rural Southern churches and in bluegrass gospel music, *He Will Set Your Fields on Fire* is a good example of a "bass lead" gospel song. On the chorus, the bass singer gets a rare chance to lead the song with the rest of the quartet joining in, as shown below. *He Will Set Your Fields on Fire* will take some practice to master.

H. M. Ballew   Mrs. L. L. Brackett

1. There's a call that rings for the one that sings, To those now gone a-stray, Say-ing, come ye men, and your load of sin, There at the al-tar lay, You don't seem to heed, and the chain of greed, Your con-science ne-ver tires, Be as-sured my friend, if you still of-fend, He will set your fields on fire.

And re-joice with Him, free from ev-'ry sin, When He sets this world on fire.

Chorus
If you don't re-tire set your fields on fire,

Bass: If you don't from sin re-tire, He will set your fields on fire, You have heard Je-sus call soon your soul must fall,

You have heard Jes-sus call, And in death you soon must fall, Now my friend, if you de-sire join the heav'n-ly choir,

friend, if you de-sire, You may join the heav'n-ly choir,

D.S. %al Fine

2. You have heard His voice, seen the soul rejoice,
   That trusted in His grace,
   You have blushed with sin as he knocked within,
   But still you hide your face,
   From the blessed Lord and His own true word,
   But still you say retire,
   Leave the downward path, kindle not His wrath,
   Or He'll set your fields on fire. *(Chorus)*

3. Won't you take advice, make the sacrifice,
   Completely turn from sin,
   Taking up the cross, counting pleasures dross,
   Let Jesus live within,
   When temptations come, you can face toward home,
   Your heart will never tire,
   But rejoice and pray in the last great day,
   When He sets this world on fire. *(Chorus)*

Hold to God's Unchanging Hand

Miss Jennie Wilson, who composed the words to *Hold to God's Unchanging Hand,* was a remarkable woman who spent most of her fifty-six years in a wheel chair. Born in 1857 on a farm near South Whitley, Indiana, she was stricken with a spinal sickness at the age of four that left her an invalid. Never attending school, she studied at home where she received some training in music. She is said to have written over 2,200 poems.

Jennie Wilson   **F. L. Eiland**

1. Time is filled with swift tran-si-tion, Naught of earth un-moved can stand, Build your hopes on things e-ter-nal, Hold to God's un-chang-ing hand.

Chorus

Hold to His hand, Hold to God's un-chang-ing hand, Hold to His hand, Hold to God's un-chang-ing hand, Build your hopes on things e-ter-nal, Hold to God's un-chang-ing hand.

2. Trust in Him who will not leave you,
   Whatsoever years may bring,
   If by earthly friends forsaken,
   Still more closely to Him cling. *(Chorus)*

3. Covet not this world's vain riches,
   That so rapidly decay,
   Seek to gain the heavenly treasures,
   They will never pass away. *(Chorus)*

4. When your journey is completed,
   If to God you have been true,
   Fair and bright the home in glory,
   Your enraptured soul will view. *(Chorus)*

How Beautiful Heaven Must Be

How Beautiful Heaven Must Be by Mrs. A. S. Brigewater and A. P. Bland has been popular both among gospel singers and commercial country musicians as well. Chosen by Grand Ole Opry star Uncle Dave Macon as his theme song, it was also carved on his tombstone.

Mrs. A. S. Bridgewater   A. P. Bland

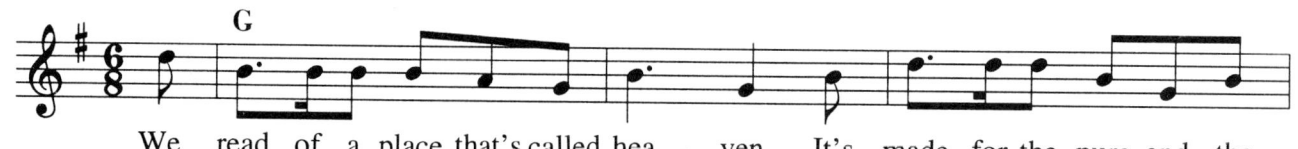

We read of a place that's called hea - ven, It's made for the pure and the

free, _____ These truths in God's Word He hath giv - en, How beau - ti - ful hea- ven must

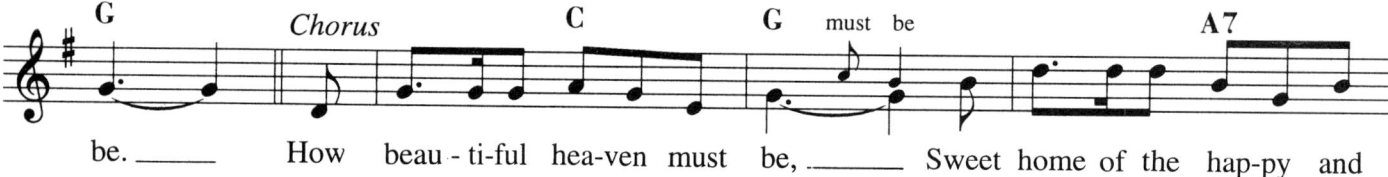

be. _____ How beau - ti - ful hea-ven must be, _____ Sweet home of the hap-py and

free,___ Fair ha-ven of rest for the wear - y, How beau-ti-ful hea-ven must be. ____

2. In heaven no drooping nor pining,
   No wishing for elsewhere to be,
   God's light is forever there shining,
   How beautiful heaven must be. *(Chorus)*

3. Pure waters of life there are flowing,
   And all who will drink may be free,
   Rare jewels of splendor are glowing,
   How beautiful heaven must be. *(Chorus)*

4. The angels so sweetly are singing,
   Up there by the beautiful sea,
   Sweet chords from their gold harps are ringing,
   How beautiful heaven must be. *(Chorus)*

I Feel Like Traveling On

William Hunter, D. D.

William Hunter, D. D.

2. Its glit'ring towers the sun outshine,
   I feel like traveling on,
   That heav'nly mansion shall be mine,
   I feel like traveling on. *(Chorus)*

3. Let others seek a home below,
   I feel like traveling on,
   Which flames devour, or waves o'er flow,
   I feel like traveling on. *(Chorus)*

4. Be mine a happier lot to own,
   I feel like traveling on,
   A heav'nly mansion near the throne,
   I feel like traveling on. *(Chorus)*

5. The Lord has been so good to me,
   I feel like traveling on,
   Until that blessed home I see,
   I feel like traveling on. *(Chorus)*

I Have Found the Way

I *Have Found the Way* has been popular in country music as performed by The Blue Sky Boys and Lester Flatt, Earl Scruggs, and the Foggy Mountain Boys. It was composed by Rev. L. E. Green and Adger M. Pace. Pace, from Pelzer, South Carolina, was born on August 13, 1882 and went on to become an important force in gospel music. A singer, composer, and singing-school teacher, he also served as music editor for Vaughn Publishing Company and was the first president of the National Singing Convention.

Rev. L. E. Green   Adger M. Pace

2. I will never fear,
   While Jesus is so near,
   I will bravely meet the foe,
   Happy song I'll sing,
   In honor to the King,
   And to glory onward go. *(Chorus)*

3. To the journey's end,
   Led by a faithful Friend,
   Nevermore is sin to roam,
   By the way called straight,
   I'll reach the golden gate,
   Of the soul's eternal home. *(Chorus)*

I Will Arise

Few folk songs can claim as varied and complex a history as *I Will Arise*. George Pullen Jackson, the authority on religious folk songs, thinks the chorus of *I Will Arise* is probably of camp meeting origin. The verses were composed by Robert Robinson (1735-1790), an English hymnist. The first verse ("Come Thou Fount . . .") has become what is called a "floating verse" and has "floated" into such as *Nettleton* or *Singer's Call, Glad News* or *We'll Land on Shore, Olney, We'll Join Heart and Hand, We'll Pass Over Jordan, I Hope to Gain the Promised Land,* and *Palms of Victory*.

The melody of *I Will Arise* has been popular in the South for over 150 years. Pieces of the tune have been found in Jackson's "Spiritual Folk Songs of Early America" (p. 233) under such titles as *Humble Penitent, Hayden, Bozrah,* and *New Orleans*. Fragments of the tune have also appeared in secular songs like *The Bird Song, Oh Love It is a Killing Thing,* and *When I First Left Old Ireland*.

Another scholar of religious folk songs, Annabell Morris Buchanan, has found evidence that the melody of *I Will Arise* is a descendent of a Scottish tune named *Hynde Horn* which dates back to the 13th century or earlier.

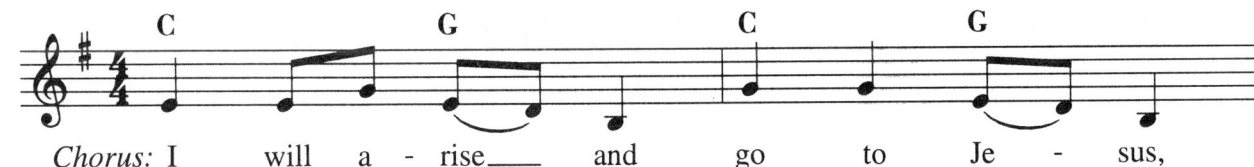

Chorus: I will a - rise___ and go to Je - sus,

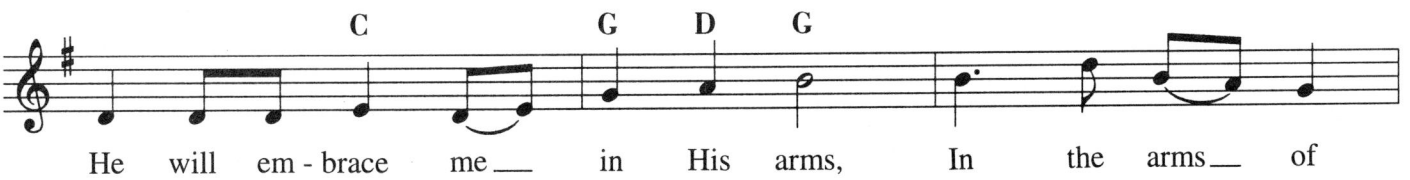

He will em - brace me ___ in His arms, In the arms ___ of

my dear Sav - ior, Oh, there are ___ ten ___ thou - sand charms.

1. Come Thou Fount of every blessing,
   Tune my heart to sing Thy grace,
   Streams of mercy never ceasing,
   Call for songs of loudest praise. *(Chorus)*

2. Teach me some melodious sonnet,
   Sung by flaming tongues above,
   Praise the mount, I'm fixed upon it,
   Mount of Thy redeeming love. *(Chorus)*

3. Here I'll raise my Ebenezer,
   Hither to Thy grace I'm come,
   And I hope by Thy good pleasure,
   Safely to arrive at home. *(Chorus)*

4. Jesus sought me when a stranger,
   Wandering from the fold of God,
   He to rescue me from danger,
   Interposed His precious blood. *(Chorus)*

I Will Never Turn Back

Found in a 1918 shaped note hymn book entitled "Revival Melodies," *I Will Never Turn Back* bore this notation: "This little hymn is free to all publishers who use it to the glory of God and His Son, our Savior."

R. N. Graham

R. N. Graham

2. Of His love I will sing every day,
   Yes, I'll sing of His wondrous power to save,
   For my Saviour is leading the way,
   To those mansions of glory above. *(Chorus)*

3. In His service each day may I be,
   Leading sinners to Jesus to be healed,
   Through the blood flowing from Calvary,
   Till the light of His love they behold. *(Chorus)*

If I Could Hear My Mother Pray Again

If I Could Hear My Mother Pray Again is a sentimental religious song composed by John W. Vaughn and James Rowe. Born in Devonshire, England, James Rowe must be counted among the most prolific lyricists gospel music has yet produced. He composed over 20,000 hymn-poems and published them with nearly every hymn book publisher in America. Among his well-known compositions is *Love Lifted Me*.

Ample testimony to the continued popularity of *If I Could Hear My Mother Pray Again* occurred at a recent music program I helped put on at a home for senior citizens in Black Mountain, North Carolina. An elderly woman came up to the stage after the program and asked to borrow a guitar. Without hesitation, she launched into *If I Could Hear My Mother Pray Again*.

James Rowe   **J. W. Vaughan**

2. She used to pray that I on Jesus would rely,
   And always walk the shining gospel way,
   So trusting still His love I seek that home above,
   Where I shall meet my mother some glad day. *(Chorus)*

3. Within the old home-place, here patient, smiling face,
   Was always spreading comfort, hope and cheer,
   And when she used to sing to her eternal King,
   It was the songs the angels loved to hear. *(Chorus)*

4. Her work on earth is done, the life-crown has been won,
   And she will be at rest with Him above,
   And some glad morning, she I know will welcome me,
   To that eternal home of peace and love. *(Chorus)*

I'll Be No Stranger There

Born in Belmont, Louisiana, on August 25, 1879, Arthus B. Sebren was only eleven years old when he attended his first singing-school. From then on he was involved with gospel music. He studied under such distinguished teachers as F. L. Eiland (*Hold to God's Unchanging Hand*) and Emmett S. Dean (*Just Over in the Gloryland*) and was known as one of the great gospel singers and teachers of his time. He sang and managed quartets for the Trio Music Company, the Quartet Music Company, the James D. Vaughn Company and the Sebren Music Company. *I'll Be No Stranger There* makes such a fine quartet number that you may find it difficult to stop singing it.

J. H. Alcon

A. B. Sebren

be   no   stran - ger   there,   I'll   be   no   stran - ger   there,   I'll

be   no   stran - ger   there,______   When   all   the   saved   come

from   their   grave,   I'll   be   no   stran - ger   there.

2. The Lord will call (the Lord will call)
        both great and small (both great and small),
  To mansions bright (to mansions bright)
        and fair (so bright and fair),
  To heaven above (to heaven above)
        where all is love (where all is love),
  I'll be no stran (I'll be no stranger) ger there (no stranger there). *(Chorus)*

3. My path is bright (my path is bright)
        my burdens light (my burdens light),
  I have a home (I have a home)
        up there (a home up there),
  I'll sing His praise (I'll sing His praise)
        through countless days (through countless days),
  I'll be no stran (I'll be no stranger) ger there (no stranger there). *(Chorus)*

4. My Savior stands (my Savior stands)
        with outstretched hands (with outstretched hands),
  He's calling me (He's calling me)
        up there (calling up there),
  His voice I hear (His voice I hear)
        I have no fear (I have no fear),
  I'll be no stran (I'll be no stranger) ger there (no stranger there). *(Chorus)*

Jesus, Savior, Pilot Me

The Rev. Edward Hopper was the Presbyterian minister of New York Harbor's Church of Sea and Land. Often composing hymns for the sailors of his church, he anonymously published *Jesus, Savior, Pilot Me* in "The Sailor's Magazine" in 1871. The tune was later written by John Edgar Gould who had edited numerous hymnals while managing a music store in New York. Gould later moved to Philadelphia and stories tell that he composed the music to *Jesus, Savior, Pilot Me* on the night before he sailed for Africa. The hymn had been sung for nine years before it was finally discovered that Edward Hopper had written it.

Edward Hopper   **John E. Gould**

1. Je - sus, Sav - ior, pi - lot me O - ver life's tem - pest - uous

sea, Un-known waves be - fore me roll, Hid - ing rock and treach-'rous

shoal, Chart and com - pass came_ from Thee, Je - sus, Sav - ior, pi - lot me.

2. As a mother stills her child,
   Thou canst hush the ocean wild,
   Boisterous waves obey Thy will,
   When Thou sayest to them "Be still,"
   Wondrous Sovereign of the sea,
   Jesus, Savior, pilot me.

3. When at last I near the shore,
   And the fearful breakers roar,
   'Twixt me and peaceful rest,
   Then while leaning on Thy breast,
   May I hear Thee say to me,
   "Fear not, I will pilot thee."

Floyd County, Virginia
American Folklife Center
Photo by Pat Mullen

Just A Closer Walk With Thee

No one knows who composed *Just A Closer Walk With Thee*. We do know that it became a standard in gospel music after it was recorded by country music star Red Foley in 1950. While most gospel songs are written for quartet or congregational singing, *Just A Closer Walk With Thee* makes a powerful solo.

Unknown

1. I am weak, but Thou art strong,
Chorus : Just a clo - ser walk with Thee,

Je - sus, keep me from all wrong, I'll be sat - is - fied as
Grant it Je - sus is my plea, Dai - ly walk- ing close to

long, As I walk, let me walk close to Thee.
Thee, Let it be, Oh Lord, let it be.

2. Through this world of toil and snares,
   If I falter, Lord, who cares?
   Who with me my burden shares?
   None but Thee, dear Lord, none but Thee. *(Chorus)*

3. When my feeble life is o'er,
   Time for me will be no more,
   Guide my gently, safely o'er,
   To Thy kingdom shore, to Thy shore. *(Chorus)*

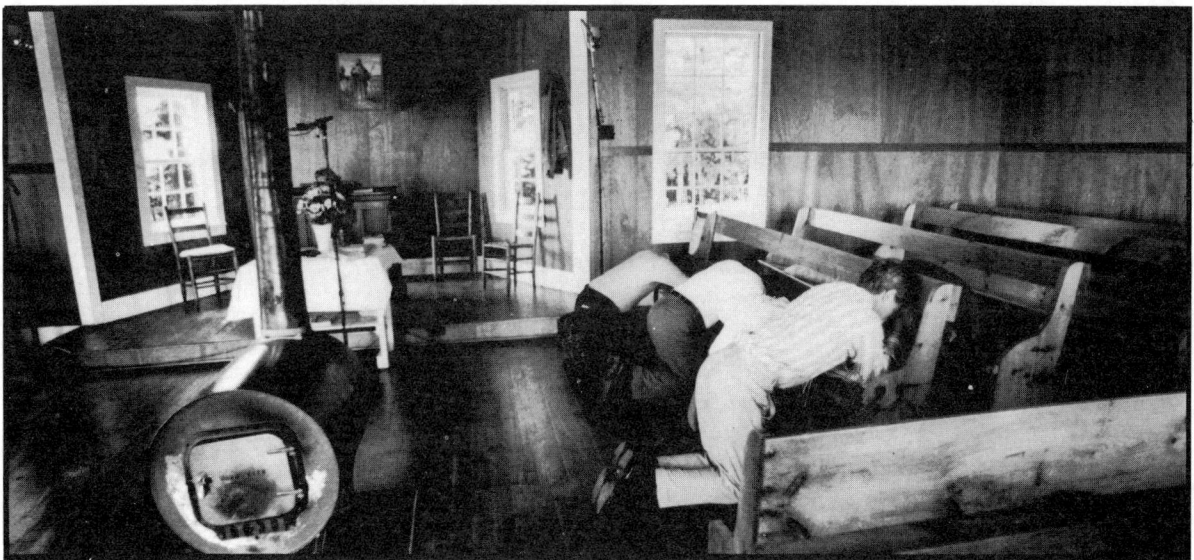

Laurel Glen Regular Baptist Church, Alleghany County, North Carolina
American Folklife Center
Photo by Lyntha Eiler

Just Over in the Gloryland

Written in 1906 by James W. Acuff and Emmett S. Dean, *Just Over in the Gloryland* has long been a favorite of old-time and bluegrass bands alike. The song is usually sung as a quartet with the lead singer singing the first and third lines solo and the bass, baritone, and tenor joining in on the second and fourth lines. On the chorus, the lead singer holds the word "over" while the harmony singers sing "over over." This song will take some practice to master.

James W. Acuff
and Emmett S. Dean

1. I've a home pre-pared where the saints a-bide, Just_ o-ver in the glo-ry -

land. And I long to be by my Sa-vior's side, Just_ o-ver in the glo-ry - land.

Chorus o-ver o-ver yes join

Just o - ver in the glo-ry-land, I'll join____ the hap-py an-gel band. Just

o-ver o-ver

o-ver in the glo-ry - land. Just o - ver in the glo-ry-land. There

yes with

with ____ the might-y host I'll stand, Just_ o-ver in the glo-ry - land.

2. I am on my way to those mansions fair,
   Just over in the gloryland,
   There to sing God's praise and His glory share,
   Just over in the gloryland. *(Chorus)*

3. What a joyful thought that my Lord I'll see,
   Just over in the gloryland,
   And with kindred saved there forever be,
   Just over in the gloryland. (Chorus)

4. With the bloodwashed throng I will shout and sing,
   Just over in the gloryland,
   Glad hosannas to Christ, the Lord and King,
   Just over in the gloryland. *(Chorus)*

Keep on the Sunny Side of Life

Ada Blenkhorn's invalid cousin always insisted that she push his wheel chair down "the sunny side of the street." It was from this that she was inspired to write the words to *Keep on the Sunny Side of Life*. The music was composed by J. Howard Entwisle and copyrighted in 1899.

Although recorded as early as 1910 on a cylinder, it was the Carter family, from Maces Springs, Virginia, who made the song popular as their theme song. The Carter's recorded it at their second session for Victor, on May 9, 1928, and again on May 8, 1935 for the American Record Company. Although the song became quite popular, it was seldom recorded by other artists, presumably because it was so closely associated with the Carter family.

Ada Blenkhorn   **J. Howard Entwisle**

1. There's a dark and a troub-led side of life, There's a bright and a sun-ny side, too, Though we meet with the dark-ness and strife,___ The sun-ny side we al-so may view. Keep on the sun-ny side, Al-ways on the sun-ny side, Keep on the sun-ny side of life, It will help us ev-'ry day, It will bright-en all the way, If we keep on the sun-ny side of life.

2. Though the storm in its fury break today,
Crushing hopes that we cherished so dear,
Storm and cloud will in time pass away,
The sun again will shine bright and clear. *(Chorus)*

3. Let us greet with a song of hope each day,
Though the moments be cloudy or fair,
Let us trust in our Savior alway,
Who keepeth every one in His care. *(Chorus)*

Kneel at the Cross

Born in 1891 in Gordon County, Georgia, Charles E. Moody once traded a shotgun for his first fiddle. By the time he started recording with the Georgia Yellow Hammers in February of 1927, he had also mastered the guitar, ukulele, banjo, and harmonica. Although he wrote some rather unusual songs such as *The Moonshine Hollow Band,* and *Song of the Doodle Bug,* Moody will be remembered as a gospel songwriter who composed such classics as *Drifting Too Far from the Shore,* and *Kneel at the Cross.*

Charles E. Moody   Charles E. Moody

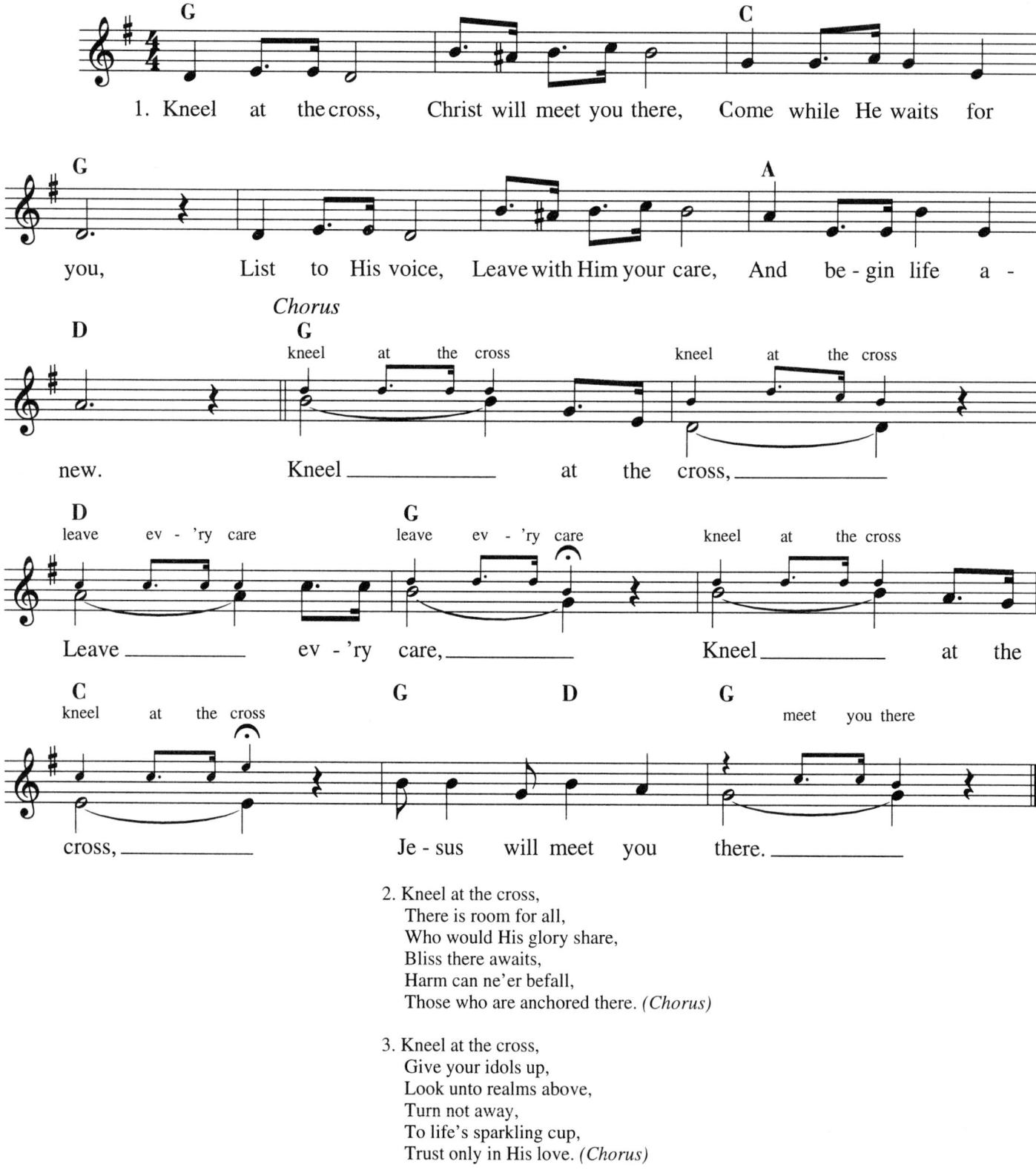

2. Kneel at the cross,
   There is room for all,
   Who would His glory share,
   Bliss there awaits,
   Harm can ne'er befall,
   Those who are anchored there. *(Chorus)*

3. Kneel at the cross,
   Give your idols up,
   Look unto realms above,
   Turn not away,
   To life's sparkling cup,
   Trust only in His love. *(Chorus)*

Leaning on the Everlasting Arms

It was in 1888 that Rev. Anthony J. Showalter composed *Leaning on the Everlasting Arms.* Born in 1858 in Cherry Grove, Pennsylvania, he gave this explanation of how he came to write *Leaning on the Everlasting Arms.* "While I was conducting a singing-school at Hartsells, Alabama, I received a letter from two of my former pupils in South Carolina, conveying the sad intelligence that on the same day each of them had buried his wife . . . I tried to console them by writing a letter that might prove helpful in their hour of sadness. Among other Scriptures I quoted this passage. 'Underneath are the everlasting arms.' Before completing the writing of this sentence, the thought came to me that the fact that we may lean on these everlasting arms and find comfort and strength, ought to be put in a song; and before finishing that letter, the words and music of the refrain were written. The manuscript was sent to Elish A. Hoffman . . .in a few days his completion of the poem was received."

Elish A. Hoffman   **Anthony J. Showalter**

2. What have I to dread, what have I to fear,
   Leaning on the everlasting arms?
   I have blessed peace with my Lord so near,
   Leaning on the everlasting arms. *(Chorus)*

3. Oh, how sweet to walk in the pilgrim's way,
   Leaning on the everlasting arms;
   Oh, how bright the path grows from day to day,
   Leaning on the everlasting arms. *(Chorus)*

Life's Railway To Heaven

*L*ife's Railway To Heaven *is commonly known as* Life Is Like A Mountain Railroad. *It was copyrighted January 18, 1890, with words credited to a Baptist preacher named M. E. Abbey and music to Charles D. Tillman from Atlanta, Georgia. However, the authors "borrowed" heavily from a poem written by Civil War era songwriter William Shakespeare Hays, who wrote songs like* Little Log Cabin In the Lane *and* Drummer Boy of Shiloh. *Hays' poem was published in 1886 and entitled* The Faithful Engineer. *It began "Life is like a crooked railroad, and the engineer is brave . . ."*

M. E. Abbey

Charles D. Tillman

1. Life is like _____ a moun-tain rail - road _____ With an

en - gi - neer that's brave; We must make _____ the run suc -

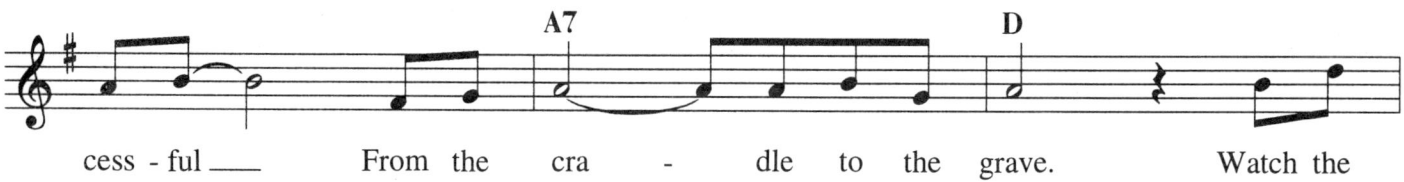

cess - ful ___ From the cra - dle to the grave. Watch the

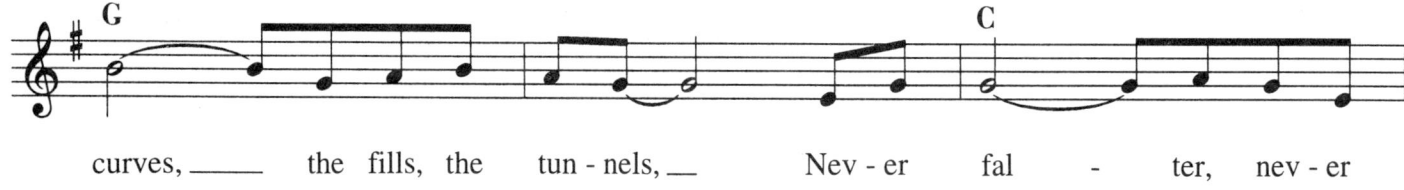

curves, _____ the fills, the tun - nels, ___ Nev - er fal - ter, nev - er

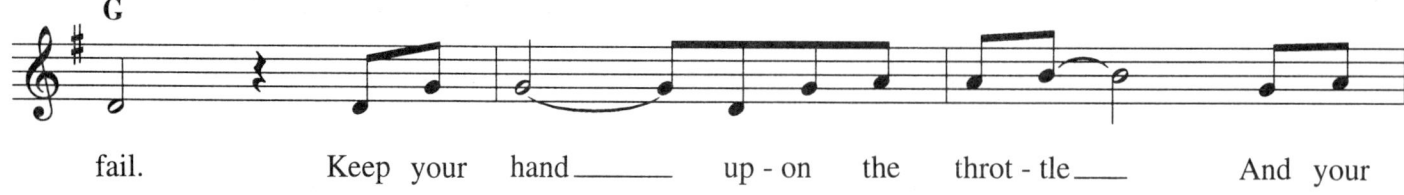

fail. Keep your hand _____ up - on the throt - tle ___ And your

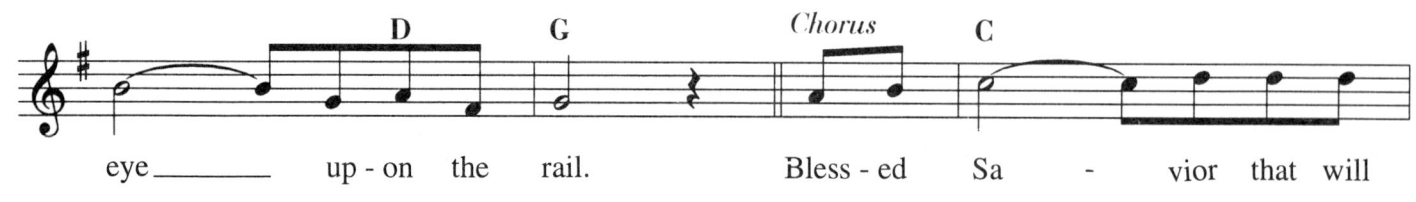

eye _____ up - on the rail. Bless - ed Sa - vior that will

guide us___ 'Till we reach_____ that bliss-**ful** shore, Where the

an - gels wait to join us___ In Thy praise___ for - ev - er___ more.___

2. As you roll up grades of trial, you will cross the bridges of strife,
See that Christ is your conductor on the lightning train of life,
Always mindful of obstruction, do your duty, never fail,
Keep your hand upon the throttle and your eye upon the rail. *(Chorus)*

3. As you roll across the trestle look for storm or wind and rain,
On a curve or fill or trestle they will almost ditch your train,
Put your trust alone in Jesus, never falter, never fail,
Keep your hand upon the throttle and your eye upon the rail. (Chorus)

4. As you roll across the trestle, spanning Jordan's swelling tide,
You'll behold the union depot into which your train will glide,
There you'll meet the superintendent God the Father, God the Son,
With a hearty, joyous plaudit, weary pilgrim, welcome home. *(Chorus)*

Baptism in Holston River
Slabtown, Smith County, Virginia
Reproduced from the collection of the Library of Congress

Lord, I'm Coming Home

Lord, I'm Coming Home was written by William J. Kirkpatrick and copyrighted in 1892. The usual bluegrass arrangement of the song as recorded by Jimmy Martin and Charlie Moore, is for the lead singer to sing the first and third lines of the verses solo and for the harmony singers to chime in on the second and fourth lines.

William J. Kirkpatrick   William J. Kirkpatrick

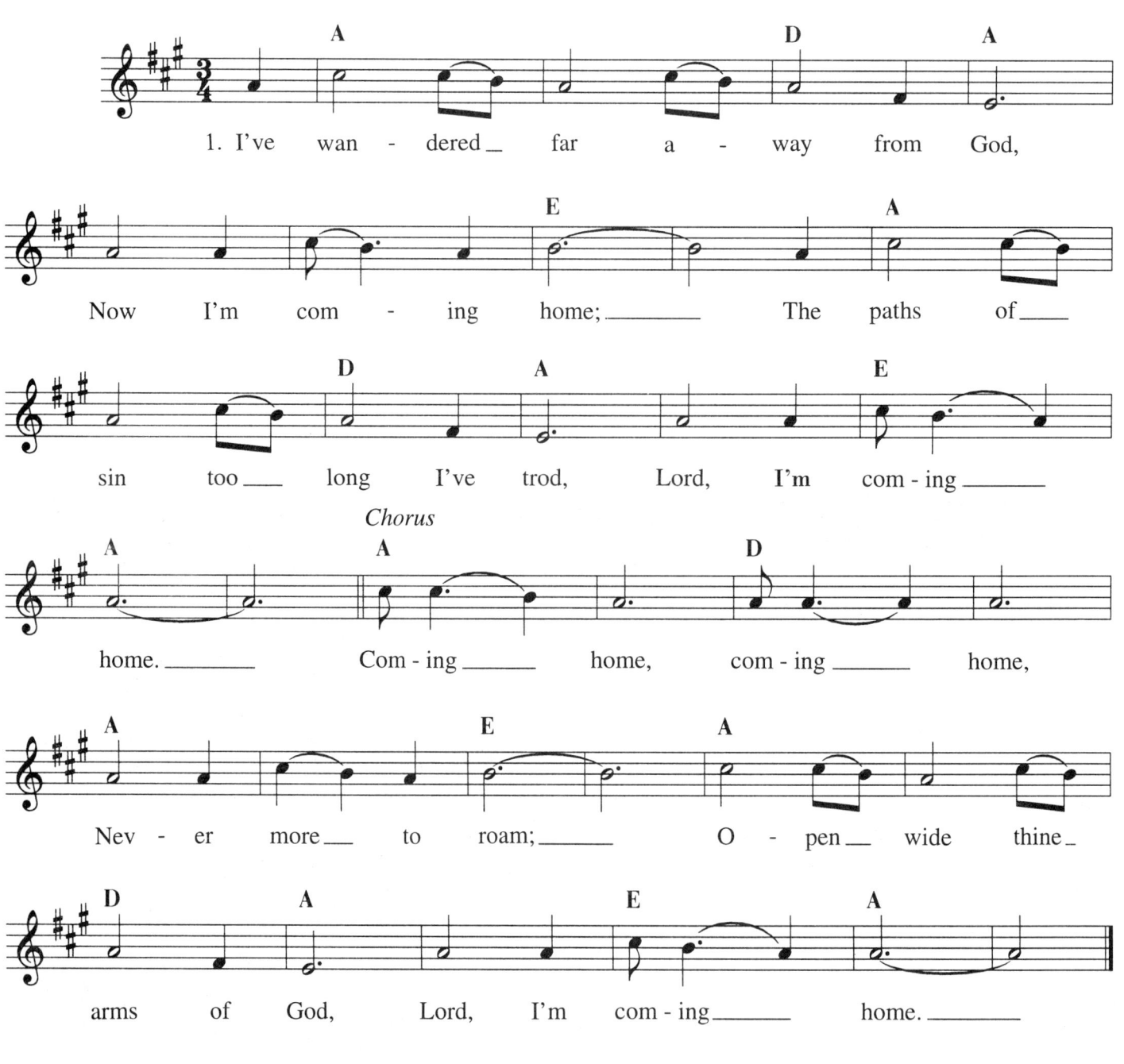

2. I've wasted many precious years,
   Now I'm coming home;
   I now repent with bitter tears,
   Lord, I'm coming home. *(Chorus)*

3. I'm tired of sin and strayin', Lord,
   Now I'm coming home;
   I'll trust Thy love, believe Thy word,
   Lord, I'm coming home. *(Chorus)*

Laurel Glen Regular Baptist Church, Alleghany County, North Carolina
American Folklife Center
Photo by Lyntha Eiler

Methodist Pie

*M*ethodist Pie is a comical gospel song of unknown authorship. This version comes from the singing of Bradley Kincaid, known as the "Kentucky Mountain Boy." Bradley remembered that it was written ". . .after going to Camp Nelson, Kentucky to hear circuit-rider preachers at old-fashioned Methodist camp meetings."

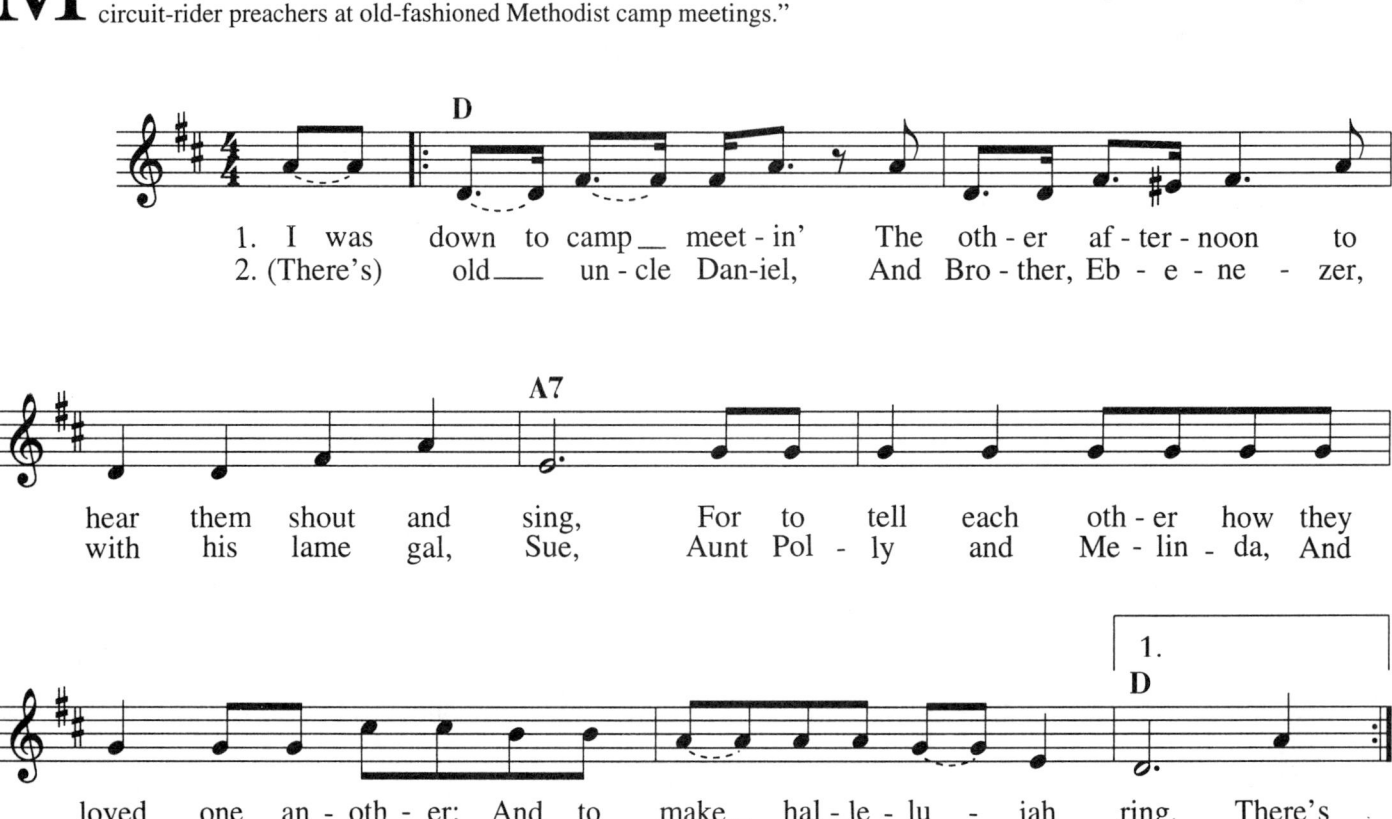

1. I was down to camp meet-in' The oth-er af-ter-noon to
2. (There's) old un-cle Dan-iel, And Bro-ther, Eb-e-ne-zer,

hear them shout and sing, For to tell each oth-er how they
with his lame gal, Sue, Aunt Pol-ly and Me-lin-da, And

loved one an-oth-er; And to make hal-le-lu-jah ring. There's
old Mo-ther Bren-der, Well, I nev-er seen a hap-pi-er

crew. Oh, lit-tle chil-dren, I be-lieve,

Oh, lit-tle chil-dren, I be-lieve, Oh, lit-tle

chil-dren, I be-lieve, I'm a Meth-od-ist till I die, I'm a

Meth-od-ist, a Meth-od- ist, "Tis my be-lief, Meth-od-ist till I die, When

old grim Death comes a -knock - ing at the door, I'm a Meth-od-ist till I die.

2. Well, they all go there,
   For to have a good time,
   And to eat that grub so sly,
   Have applesauce butter,
   With sugar in the gourd,
   And a great Methodist Pie.

   Well, you ought to hear the ringing,
   When they all get to singing,
   That good old Bye and Bye,
   See Jimmy McGee in the top of a tree,
   Saying "How is this for high?" *(Chorus)*

3. Then they catch a hold of hands,
   And march around the ring,
   Kept a-singing all the while,
   You'd think it was a cyclone,
   Coming through the air,
   You could hear them shout a half a mile.

   Then the bell rings loud,
   And the great big crowd,
   Breaks ranks and up they fly,
   While I took board,
   On the sugar in the gourd,
   And I cleaned up the Methodist Pie. *(Chorus)*

Laurel Glen Regular Baptist Church, Alleghany County, North Carolina
American Folklife Center
Photo by Terry Eiler

Oh, Those Tombs

Oh, Those Tombs was written by William M. Golden, from Mississippi, and bears this chilling note: "composed after a walk through the city of the dead." Golden was also the composer of the popular gospel song *A Beautiful Life*. Bill Bolick, who recorded *Oh, Those Tombs* with his brother Earl as The Blue Sky Boys, learned it from his father who found it in a shape-note hymnal with the notation that it was composed in the late 1880s.

William M. Golden

William M. Golden

2. Ev-'ry voice from the tombs seemed to whisper and say,
   "Living man, you must soon follow me,"
   And I thought as I looked on these cold marble slabs,
   What a dark, lonely place that must be. *(Chorus)*

3. Then I came to the place where my mother was laid,
   And in silence I stood by her tomb,
   And her voice seemed to say in a low, gentle tone,
   "I am safe with my Savior at home." *(Chorus)*

Old-Time Religion

The same qualities of repetition and simplicity that made *Old-Time Religion* so popular at camp meeting revivals among both blacks and whites, insure its continued popularity today. Few other songs can rival it for getting people to sing.

Among the first to collect *Old-Time Religion* was the Rev. Charles D. Tillman who later composed *Life's Railway to Heaven.* At a revival in the late 1880s, Tillman first heard the song and transcribed it from the singing of a Negro blacksmith named Rawlings. In addition to inspiring enthusiastic response from singers, *Old-Time Religion* has been played on the fiddle as a lively square dance tune.

1. Give me that old time re - li - gion, give me that old time re -

li - gion, give me that old time re - li - gion, It's good e-nough for me.

2. It was good for Paul and Silas,
   It was good for Paul and Silas,
   It was good for Paul and Silas,
   It's good enough for me.

3. It was good for our mothers,
   It was good for our mothers,
   It was good for our mothers,
   It's good enough for me.

4. Makes me love everybody,
   Makes me love everybody,
   Makes me love everybody,
   It's good enough for me.

5. It was precious to our fathers,
   It was precious to our fathers,
   It was precious to our fathers,
   It's good enough for me.

6. It will take us all to heaven,
   It will take us all to heaven,
   It will take us all to heaven,
   It's good enough for me.

Rev. Robert Akers Tent Revival, Galax, Virginia
American Folklife Center
Photo by Terry Eiler

On the Sea of Life

On the Sea of Life is a powerful gospel song written by George W. Sebren and T. S. Sloan. Sebren sang lead in J. D. Vaughn's first gospel quartet which was organized in 1910. He later formed his own publishing company in Asheville, North Carolina. The earliest known version of *On the Sea* was in 1928 on Columbia by the Ropers Mountain singers.

George W. Sebren

T. S. Sloan

2. We've a Captain brave and true,
   Who will guide us o'er the blue,
   And will shield us when the storms hover nigh,
   He can still the angry wave,
   And from evil He can save,
   If we'll trust Him and His loving promise try. *(Chorus)*

3. Many millions now abide,
   In that home beyond the sky,
   Where the ransomed pilgrims wait free from care,
   There is room on board for all,
   Who will heed the Captain's call,
   And take ship for heaven's country bright and fair. *(Chorus)*

Our Meeting is Over

Since the late 1800s, *Our Meeting is Over* has been used to close many camp meeting revivals and religious services. Its "gapped" scale and haunting melody can still be heard in backwood churches in the South. Also known as *Glad News* or *We'll Land on the Shore,* it has been collected with the "floating" verse that begins "Come thou fount of every blessing. . ."

1. Fa - thers, now our __ meet - ing is o - ver, Sure - ly we __ must part, And if I nev - er __ see you a - gain __ I'll love you in __ my heart.

Chorus

Yes, we'll land on the shore,_ Yes, we'll land_____ on __ the shore, Lord, we'll land on the shore _ and be saved for-ev - er more.

2. Mothers, now our meeting is over,
   Surely we must part,
   And if I never see you again,
   I'll love you in my heart. *(Chorus)*

3. Sisters, now our meeting is over,
   Surely we must part,
   And if I never see you again,
   I'll love you in my heart. *(Chorus)*

4. Brothers, now our meeting is over,
   Surely we must part,
   And if I never see you again,
   I'll love you in my heart. *(Chorus)*

Palms of Victory

lso known as *Deliverance Will Come, Palms of Victory* was published in the 1855 edition of "The Social Harp" with the notation Henry F. Chandler, 1854. The chorus of this version is similar to the one below, but included the common floating verse "Come thou fount . . ." The more popular version, given below, was credited to John B. Matthias and appeared in the 1870s. The melody of *Palms of Victory* was later borrowed for the Southern protest song entitled *Pans of Biscuits*. The words to the chorus are "Pans of biscuits, bowls of gravy/Pans of biscuits we shall have."

John B. Matthias   John B. Matthias

1. I___ saw a way-worn trav-'ler, In tat-tered gar-ments clad, And_

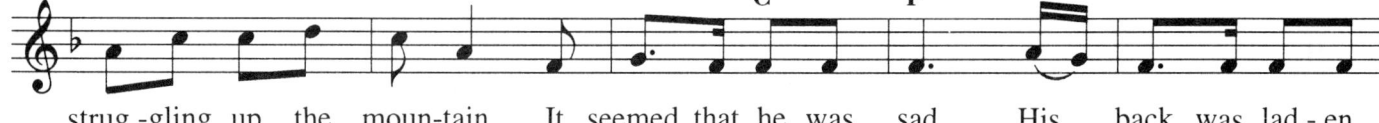

strug-gling up the moun-tain, It seemed that he was sad. His_ back was lad-en

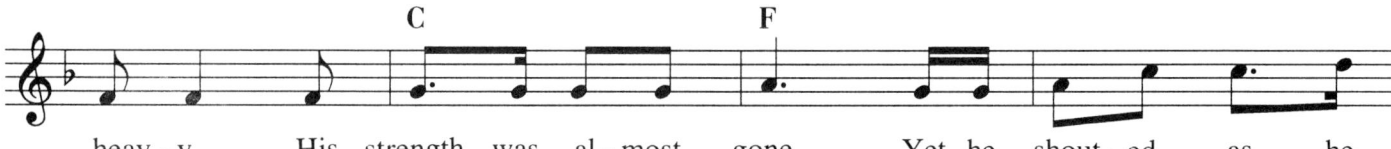

heav-y, His strength was al-most gone, Yet he shout-ed as he

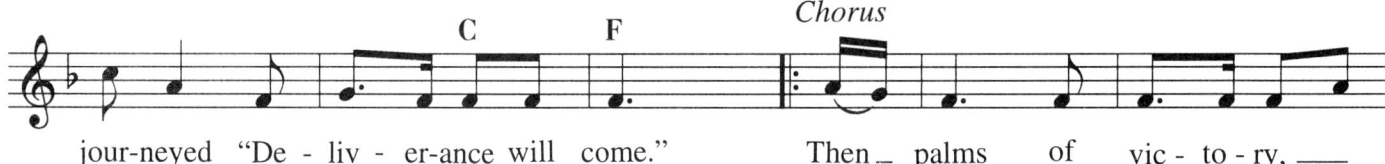

Chorus

jour-neyed "De-liv-er-ance will come." Then_ palms of vic-to-ry, ___

Crowns of glo-ry, Palms of vic-to-ry I ___ shall _ wear.

2. The summer sun was shining,
   The sweat was on his brow,
   His garments worn and dusty,
   His step seemed very slow.
   But he kept pressing onward,
   For he was wending home,
   Still shouting as he journeyed
   "Deliverance will come." *(Chorus)*

3. The songsters in the arbor,
   That stood beside the way,
   Attracted his attention,
   In visiting his delay.
   His watchword being "Onward!"
   He stopped his ears and ran,
   Still shouting as he journeyed
   "Deliverance will come." *(Chorus)*

4. I saw him in the evening,
   The sun was bending low,
   He'd overtopped the mountain,
   And reached the vale below.
   He saw the golden city,
   His everlasting home,
   And shouted loud "Hosanna,
   Deliverance will come." *(Chorus)*

5. While gazing on that city,
   Just o'er that narrow flood,
   A band of holy angels,
   Came from the throne of God.
   They bore him on their pinions
   Safe o'er the dashing foam,
   And joined him in his triumph—
   Deliverance will come. *(Chorus)*

6. I heard the song of triumph,
   They sang upon that shore,
   Saying "Jesus has redeemed us,
   To suffer nevermore."
   Then casting his eyes backward,
   On the race which he had run,
   He shouted loud "Hosanna,
   Deliverance will come." *(Chorus)*

Pass Me Not

It was in 1868 that Dr. William H. Doane asked blind poet and composer Fanny J. Crosby to write a hymn on the theme "Pass me not, O gentle Savior." Blinded by an accident in early childhood, she became a gifted and famous composer and is said to have written over 8,000 poems. Her composition of *Pass Me Not* was set to music by Doane and first published in his "Songs of Devotion" in 1870. It was popularized by Ira D. Sankey at the revivals held by evangelist Dwight L. Moody.

Fanny J. Crosby   William H. Doane

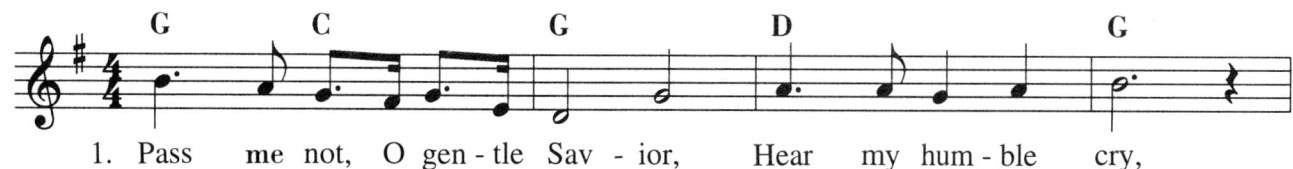

1. Pass me not, O gen-tle Sav-ior, Hear my hum-ble cry,

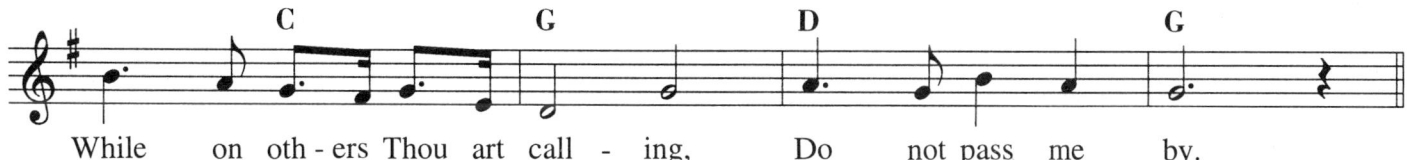

While on oth-ers Thou art call-ing, Do not pass me by.

Chorus

Sav-ior, Sav-ior, Hear my hum-ble cry,

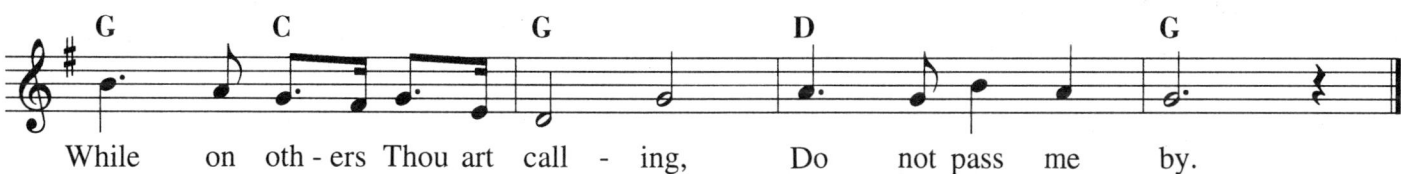

While on oth-ers Thou art call-ing, Do not pass me by.

2. Let me at a throne of mercy,
   Find a sweet relief,
   Kneeling there in deep contrition,
   Help my unbelief. *(Chorus)*

3. Trusting only in Thy merit,
   Would I seek Thy face,
   Heal my wounded, broken spirit,
   Save me by Thy grace. *(Chorus)*

4. Thou the Spring of all my comfort,
   More than life to me,
   Whom have I on earth beside Thee?
   Whom in heaven but Thee? *(Chorus)*

Pleasant Grove Union Baptist Church
Alleghany County, North Carolina
American Folklife Center
Photo by Terry Eiler

Poor Wayfaring Stranger

P*oor Wayfaring Stranger* is a religious folk song that has been passed down by the hands of sacred and secular singers from both the white and black tradition. The tune seems to be a variant of ballads such as *Barbara Allen, In Old Virginny, Come All You Fair and Tender Ladies, Dear Companion,* and *George Reilly.* The earliest known version of the tune in print appeared under the title *Judgment* in Ananias Davisson's "Kentucky Harmony" published in 1816.

2. I know dark clouds will gather round me,
    I know my way is rough and steep,
    Yet beauteous fields lie just before me,
    Where God's redeem'd their vigils keep.

    I'm going there to see my mother,
    She said she'd meet me when I come,
    I'm only going over Jordan,
    I'm only going over home.

3. I'll soon be freed from every trial,
    My body sleep in the church-yard,
    I'll drop the cross of self-denial,
    And enter on my great reward.

    I'm going there to see my Savior,
    To sing His praise forevermore,
    I'm only going over Jordan,
    I'm only going over home.

Precious Memories

It is not hard to understand the continued popularity of *Precious Memories* both in gospel music and in commercial country music and bluegrass as well. When the going gets rough, how many times have our own thoughts turned back to cherished memories of family and home?

J. B. F. Wright, the composer of *Precious Memories,* was born in Tennessee on February 21, 1877. Unlike many composers of gospel music, Wright's background never included formal music training. Even in his early years he wrote solely from inspiration. As he has said, "The words come spontaneously, flowing into place when I feel the divine urge."

J. B. F. Wright   J. B. F. Wright

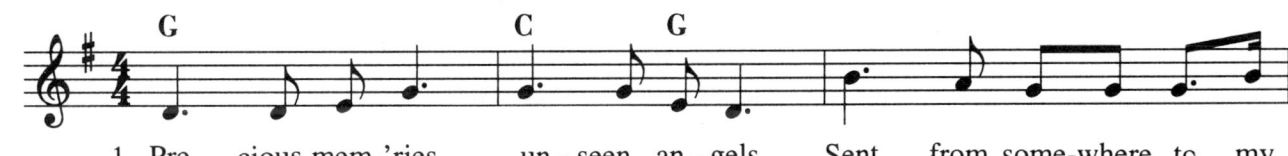

1. Pre - cious mem-'ries,   un - seen an - gels,   Sent   from some-where to   my

soul,   How   they lin-ger,   ev - er near me,   And   the sa-cred past un-fold.

Chorus

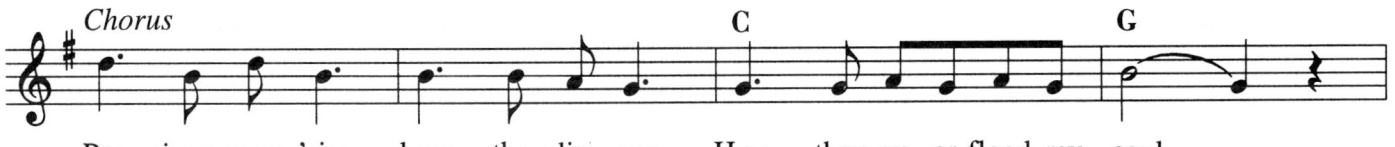

Pre - cious mem-'ries,   how   they lin - ger,   How   they ev - er flood my   soul,___

In   the still-ness   of   the mid-night,   Pre - cious, sa- cred scenes un-fold.

2. Precious father, loving mother,
   Fly across the lonely years,
   And old home scenes of my childhood,
   In fond memory appears. *(Chorus)*

3. In the stillness of the midnight,
   Echoes from the past I hear,
   Old-time singing, gladness bringing,
   From that lovely land somewhere. *(Chorus)*

4. As I travel on life's pathway,
   Knowing not what the years may hold,
   As I ponder, hope grows fonder,
   Precious mem'ries flood my soul. *(Chorus)*

Rock of Ages

Legend has it that *Rock of Ages* was composed in a cleft of rock during a violent storm by Augustas M. Toplady and written down on a six of diamonds that he had in his pocket at the time. What he was doing with a card in his pocket we would be very curious to know. Skeptics of this legend point to an article written by Toplady in October of 1775 where the poem later known as *Rock of Ages* first appeared. In the article, Toplady explains the impossibility of paying one's debts to God and calculated that if a man sinned every day, hour, minute and second, an eighty year-old man would have committed 2,522,800,000 sins. The tune of *Rock of Ages* was written by Thomas Hastings and first appeared in 1830.

Augustus M. Toplady   **Thomas Hastings**

1. Rock of A - ges, cleft for me, Let me hide my - self in

Thee, Let the wa - ter and the blood, From Thy wound - ed side which

flowed, Be of sin the dou - ble cure, Save from wrath and make me pure.

2. Could my tears forever flow,
   Could my zeal no languor know,
   Those for sin could not atone,
   Thou must save, and Thou alone,
   In my hand no price I bring,
   Simply to Thy cross I cling.

3. While I draw this fleeting breath,
   When my eyes shall close in death,
   When I rise to worlds unknown,
   And behold Thee on Thy throne,
   Rock of Ages, cleft for me,
   Let me hide myself in Thee.

Photo by Wayne Erbsen

Shake Hands With Mother Again

The hope of reuniting with loved ones in heaven is a powerful theme in gospel music. Equally important to the sentimental songs of the 1890s were songs of "Mother." W. A. Berry combines these two themes in *Shake Hands With Mother Again.*

W. A. Berry   W. A. Berry

1. If I should be liv-ing when Je-sus comes, And know the day and___ the

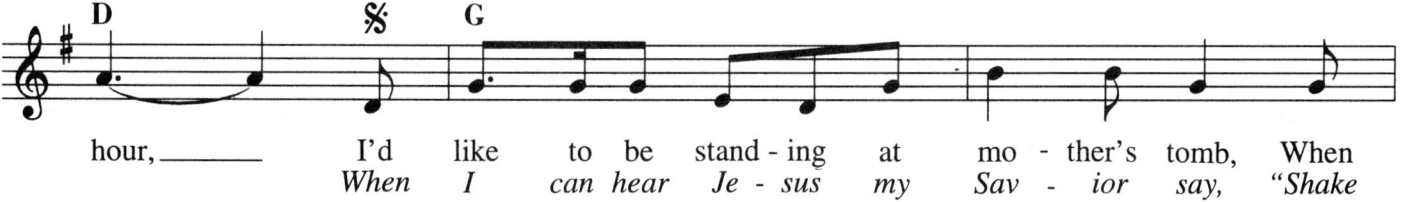

hour,_____ I'd like to be stand-ing at mo-ther's tomb, When
When I can hear Je-sus my Sav-ior say, "Shake

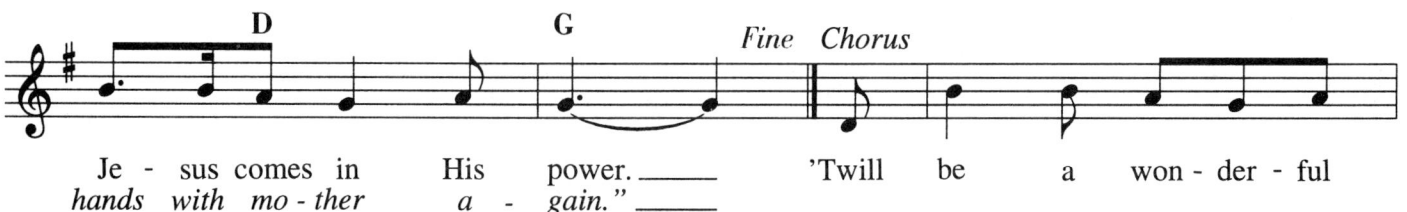

Je-sus comes in His power._____ 'Twill be a won-der-ful
hands with mo-ther a - gain." _____

hap - py day, Up there on the gol - den strand,_____

2. I'd like to say "Mother, this is your boy,
   You left when you went away,
   And now my dear mother it gives me great joy,
   To see you again today." *(Chorus)*

3. There's coming a time when I can go home,
   To meet my loved ones there,
   There I can see Jesus upon His throne,
   In that bright city so fair. *(Chorus)*

4. There'll be no sorrow, no pain to bear,
   In that home beyond the sky,
   A glorious thought when we all get there,
   We never will say "good bye." *(Chorus)*

Shall We Gather at the River?

*S*hall We Gather at the River? is an old-time gospel song written by Robert Lowry in 1864. It was first recorded on May 10, 1927, by the Dixie Sacred Singers composed of Uncle Dave Macon, along with Sam and Kirk McGee. It was, incidentally, one of Uncle Dave's favorite hymns.

Robert Lowry   Robert Lowry

1. Shall we gath - er at the riv - er, Where bright an - gel feet have trod; —

With its crys-tal tide for - ev - er, Flow-ing by the throne of — God?

Chorus

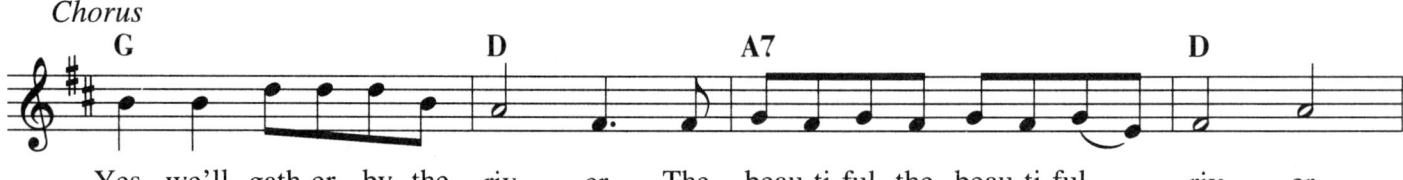

Yes, we'll gath-er by the riv - er, The beau-ti-ful, the beau-ti-ful — riv - er,

Gath-er with the saints at the riv - er, That flows by the throne of — God.

2. On the margin of the river,
    Washing up its silver spray,
    We will walk and worship ever,
    All the happy golden day. *(Chorus)*

3. There we reach the shining river,
    Lay we every burden down,
    Grace our spirits will deliver,
    And provide a robe and crown. *(Chorus)*

4. Soon we'll reach the shining river,
    Soon our pilgrimage will cease,
    Soon our happy hearts will quiver,
    With the melody of peace. *(Chorus)*

Swing Low, Sweet Chariot

(Bluegrass Version)

1. I looked o-ver Jor-dan and what did I see,____
Com-ing for to car-ry me home? A band of an-gels
com-ing af-ter me,____ Com-ing for to car-ry me home.

Chorus

Swing_ low, sweet char-i-ot,____ Com-ing for to car-ry me home, Swing

low, sweet char-i-ot,____ com-ing for to car-ry me home.

2. I'm sometimes up and I'm sometimes down,
   Coming for to carry me home,
   But still my soul feels heavenly bound,
   Coming for to carry me home. *(Chorus)*

3. If you get there before I do,
   Coming for to carry me home,
   Tell all my friends I'm coming too,
   Coming for to carry me home. *(Chorus)*

The Unclouded Day

The Unclouded Day, by Rev. J. K. Alwood, was first recorded in the early 'twenties by Homer A. Rodeheaver, who was the songleader for the evangelist Billy Sunday. It was also a hit in the 'twenties by Smith's Sacred Singers, in the 'thirties by Cliff Carlisle, and in the 'seventies by Willie Nelson.

Rev. J. K. Alwood   Rev. J. K. Alwood

1. Oh, they tell me of a home far be - yond the skies, Oh, they

tell me of a home far a - way, Oh, they tell me of a home where no

storm - clouds rise, Oh, they tell me of an un - cloud - ed day.

Oh, the land of cloud - less day, Oh, the land of an un - cloud - ed day.

2. Oh, they tell me of a home where my friends have gone,
   Oh, they tell me of that land far away,
   Where the tree of life in eternal bloom,
   Sheds its fragrance through the unclouded day. *(Chorus)*

3. Oh, they tell me of a King in His beauty there,
   And they tell me of that land far away,
   Where the tree of life in eternal bloom,
   In the city that is made of gold. *(Chorus)*

4. Oh, they tell me that He smiles on His children there,
   And His smile drives their sorrows all away,
   And they tell me that no tears ever come again,
   In that lovely land of unclouded day. *(Chorus)*

Walk in Jerusalem Just Like John

Although *Walk in Jerusalem Just Like John* probably didn't originate at a camp meeting, its structure clearly shows the influence of the camp meeting spiritual. Notice how the first line of the chorus is repeated in such a way as to almost defy you to forget the words. The verses are also in camp meeting style with the leader singing the first and third lines as a solo, and the others joining on the second and fourth lines of the refrain.

The last verse is a good example of a "floating" or "traveling" stanza, as it is called, and commonly appears in *Swing Low, Sweet Chariot*. The earliest printed appearance of this verse I have found was in "Hampton Cabin and Plantation Songs" (1874).

Walk in Jerusalem Just Like John has been popular in bluegrass music since it was recorded by Bill Monroe for Decca records on July 18, 1952. Bill remembers learning the song from a black preacher in Norwood, North Carolina many years before.

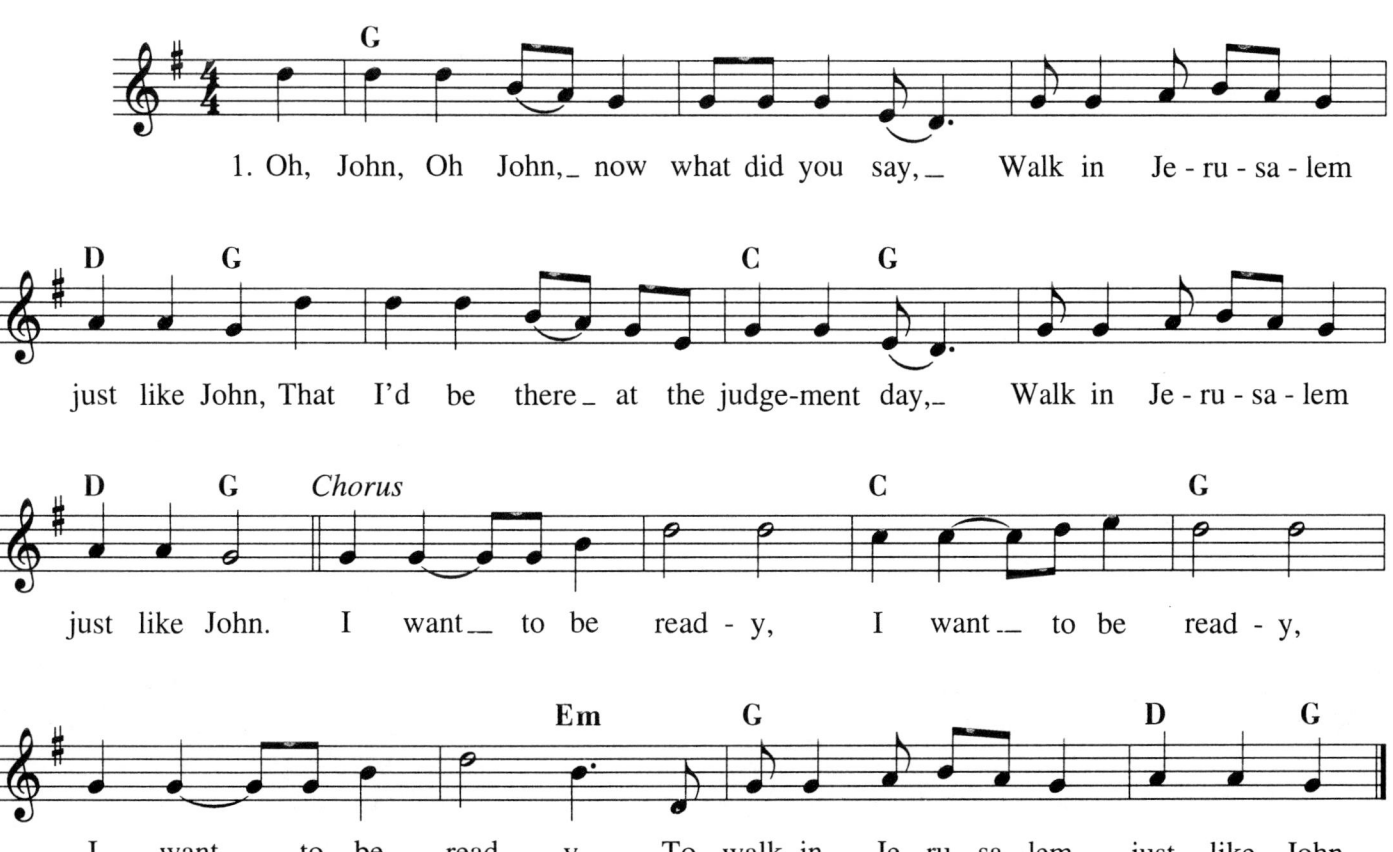

1. Oh, John, Oh John,_ now what did you say,_ Walk in Je - ru - sa - lem just like John, That I'd be there_ at the judge-ment day,_ Walk in Je - ru - sa - lem just like John. I want_ to be read - y, I want _ to be read - y, I want _ to be read - y, To walk in Je - ru - sa - lem just like John.

2. Some come crippled and some come lame,
   Walk in Jerusalem just like John,
   Some come walking in Jesus' name,
   Walk in Jerusalem just like John. *(Chorus)*

3. If you get there before I do,
   Walk in Jerusalem just like John,
   Tell all my friends I'm a-coming too,
   Walk in Jerusalem just like John. *(Chorus)*

We Are Going Down the Valley

The chorus of *We Are Going Down the Valley* leaves little doubt that it was influenced by the camp meeting spiritual. Written by Jesse Brown Pounds and J. H. Filmore, it became popular in the 1920s as recorded by Smith's Sacred Singers and Peck's Quartet. J. H. Filmore, born in Cincinnati, Ohio in 1849, joined three of his brothers to form the Filmore Brothers Music Publishing Company which published *We Are Going Down the Valley* and copyrighted it in 1905.

Jessie Brown Pounds   **J. H. Fillmore**

1. We are going down the valley one by one, With our faces toward the setting of the sun, Down the valley where the mournful cypress grows, Where the stream of death in silence onward flows.

Chorus
We are going down the valley, Going down the valley, Going toward the setting of the sun, We are going down the valley, Going down the valley, Going down the valley one by one.

2. We are going down the valley one by one,
When the labors of the weary day are done,
One by one, the cares of earth for ever past,
We shall stand upon the river brink at last. *(Chorus)*

3. We are going down the valley one by one,
Human comrade you or I will there have none,
But a tender hand will guide us lest we fall,
Christ is going down the valley with us all. *(Chorus)*

We Shall Meet Some Day

We Shall Meet Some Day, one of my personal favorites, was composed by Tillit S. Teddlie who wrote it ". . .in memory of my beloved friend, F. L. Eiland." Eiland was the composer of the music of *Hold to God's Unchanging Hand.*

Tillit S. Teddlie   Tillit S. Teddlie

1. How our hearts ache with grief as we say good bye, We shall meet some day, Where no sor-row or tears ev-er dim the eye, We shall meet some day.

Chorus

We shall meet where no storm clouds gath-er, We shall meet some day, By the ri-ver of life, spark-ling cool and clear, We shall meet some day.

2. When we've all crossed the stream with its rolling tide,
   We shall meet (we shall meet) some day,
   In that city of rest on the other side,
   We shall meet (we shall meet) some day. *(Chorus)*

3. What a glorious thought, as we say good bye,
   We shall meet (we shall meet) some day,
   In that beautiful home that's prepared on high,
   We shall meet (we shall meet) some day. *(Chorus)*

*Traveling evangelists pushing their cart between
Lafayette and Scott, LA, October 1938
Photo by Russell Lee
Reproduced from the collections of the Library of Congress*

We'll Understand It Better By and By

Charles A. Tindley, the composer of the words and music to *We'll Understand It Better By and By,* was born in slavery in Maryland on July 7, 1851. Self-educated, he mastered both Hebrew and Greek and in 1902 became pastor of a Philadelphia church. His congregation was said to number over twelve thousand.

Copyrighted in 1904, *We'll Understand It Better By and By* has become a standard not only in gospel music, but also has been performed and recorded in early country music, bluegrass, and even New Orleans jazz.

Charles A. Tindley   **Charles A. Tindley**

1. We are tossed and driven on the rest-less sea of time, Som-ber

skies and how-ling tem-pest oft suc-ceed a bright sun-shine, In that land of per-fect day, when the

mists have rolled a-way, We will un-der-stand it bet-ter by and by.

Chorus

By and by, when the morn-ing comes, All the saints of God are gath-ered home, We'll

tell the sto - ry how we've o-ver-come, For we'll un-der-stand it bet-ter by and by.

2. We are often destitute of the things that life demands,
    Want of shelter and of food—thirsty hills and barren lands,
    We are trusting in the Lord, and according to His word,
    We will understand it better by and by. *(Chorus)*

3. Trials dark on every hand, and we cannot understand,
    All the ways that God would lead us to that Blessed Promised Land,
    But He guides us with His eye and we'll follow till we die,
    For we'll understand it better by and by. *(Chorus)*

4. Temptations, hidden snares, often take us unawares,
    And our hearts are made to bleed for a thoughtless word or deed,
    And we wonder why the test when we try to do our best,
    But we'll understand it better by and by. *(Chorus)*

When the Roll is Called Up Yonder

Born in Scotland in 1882, James M. Black was kidnapped at the age of eight and brought to Canada, where he was found and taken in by an aging minister. When he was only sixteen years old, he composed the words and music to *When the Roll is Called Up Yonder.* Here is the story as told by Black: "While a teacher in a Sunday-school and president of a young people's society I one day met a girl, fourteen years old, poorly-clad and the child of a drunkard. She accepted my invitation to attend the Sunday school, and joined the young people's society. One evening, at a consecration meeting, when members answered the roll-call by repeating Scripture texts, she failed to respond. . . I longed for something suitable to sing just then, but I could find nothing in the books. We closed the meeting, and on my way home . . . the thought came to me, 'Why don't you make it?' When I reached my house the words to the first stanza came to me in full. In fifteen minutes more I had composed the other two verses. Going to the piano, I played the music just as it is found today in the hymn books, note for note, and have never dared to change a single word or a note of the piece since."

J. M. Black
J. M. Black

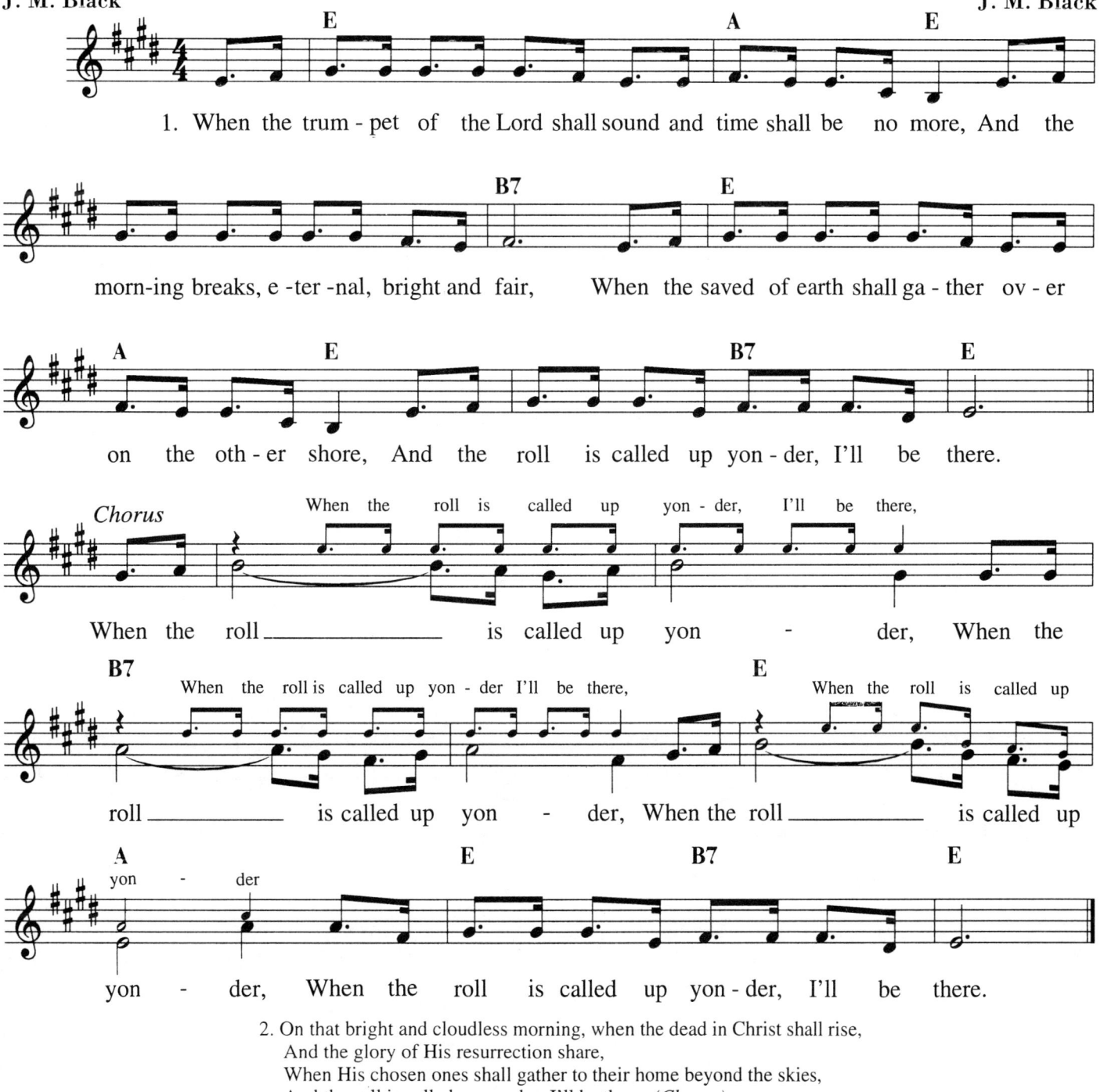

1. When the trum-pet of the Lord shall sound and time shall be no more, And the morn-ing breaks, e-ter-nal, bright and fair, When the saved of earth shall ga-ther ov-er on the oth-er shore, And the roll is called up yon-der, I'll be there.

Chorus

When the roll is called up yon-der, I'll be there,
When the roll is called up yon-der I'll be there,
When the roll is called up

When the roll ___ is called up yon - der, When the
roll ___ is called up yon - der, When the roll ___ is called up
yon - der, When the roll is called up yon - der, I'll be there.

2. On that bright and cloudless morning, when the dead in Christ shall rise,
   And the glory of His resurrection share,
   When His chosen ones shall gather to their home beyond the skies,
   And the roll is called up yonder, I'll be there. *(Chorus)*

3. Let us labor for the Master from the dawn till setting sun,
   Let us talk of all His wondrous love and care,
   Then, when all of life is over, and our work on earth is done,
   And the roll is called up yonder, I'll be there. *(Chorus)*

When They Ring the Golden Bells

They don't make them like Dion DeMarbell anymore. Born in Seville, France on July 4, 1818, it would be difficult to conceive of living a life more filled with adventure and diversity than that of Dion DeMarbell. In his 85 years he literally traveled the globe seeking his fortune. As a young man he sailed the Arctic seas on a whaling ship, fought in the U.S. Navy during the Mexican War of 1847, and acted in an American traveling opera company. Enlisting in the Sixth Michigan Infantry in the Civil War, he entertained the troops as a musician and comic, and when camped near a town, sang in the Methodist church choir. He could hold the rapt attention of a large crowd with tall tales and stories of his true-life adventures. After the Civil War, he organized a traveling troupe of actors and was later hired as a clown by Barnum and Bailey in their first circus. He then put together his own circus, which was tragically destroyed by fire. Having lost everything, Dion teamed up with Colonel William F. Cody, known as "Buffalo Bill," and his Wild West Show.

Skilled as a clown, musician, and actor, Dion was also a printer, woodcarver, magician, ventriloquist, and "one-man show." But it was as a composer that he will be remembered. In 1887, at the age of 69, he wrote *When They Ring the Golden Bells*. Unfortunately, he never earned a cent from this classic of gospel music.

Dion DeMarbell   Dion DeMarbell

1. There's a land be-yond the riv-er, That we call the sweet for-ev-er, And we

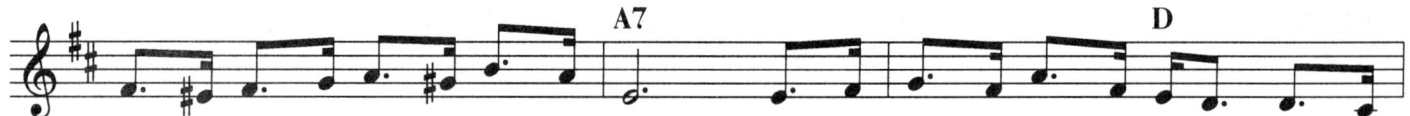

on - ly reach that shore by faith's de - cree, One by one we'll gain the por-tals, There to

dwell with the im-mor-tals, When they ring the gol - den bells for you and me.
yond the shin - ing riv - er, When they ring the gol - den bells for you and me.

Chorus

Don't you hear the bells now ring-ing? Don't you hear the an - gels sing-ing? 'Tis the

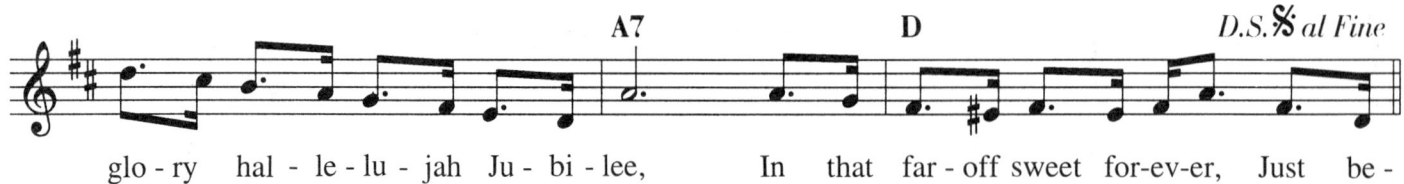

glo - ry hal - le - lu - jah Ju - bi - lee, In that far - off sweet for-ev-er, Just be -

2. When our days shall know their number,
And in death we sweetly slumber,
When the King commands the spirit to be free,
Nevermore with anguish laden,
We shall reach that lovely aiden,
When they ring the golden bells for you and me. *(Chorus)*

Lancaster, NH, February 1936
Photo by Arthur Rothstein

Where The Soul of Man Never Dies

Where The Soul of Man Never Dies, written by William M. Golden, is one of the more challenging duet gospel songs to sing. The verses are sung in normal fashion except that while the lead holds the word "soul," the tenor gets to sing "of man." On the chorus, the lead sings one set of words ("No sad . . .") and the tenor a different set of words ("Dear friends . . .").

Among the artists who have recorded this song are Hank and Audrey Williams, on MGM, and Tony Rice and Ricky Skaggs on Sugar Hill.

William M. Golden   William M. Golden

2. A rose is blooming there for me,
   Where the soul (of man) never dies.
   And I will spend eternity,
   Where the soul (of man) never dies. *(Chorus)*

3. A love light beams across the foam,
   Where the soul (of man) never dies.
   It shines to light the shores of home,
   Where the soul (of man) never dies. *(Chorus)*

4. My life will end in deathless sleep,
   Where the soul (of man) never dies.
   And everlasting joys I'll reap,
   Where the soul (of man) never dies. *(Chorus)*

5. I'm on my way to that fair land,
   Where the soul (of man) never dies.
   Where there will be no parting hand,
   Where the soul (of man) never dies. *(Chorus)*

Where We'll Never Grow Old

Born on May 2, 1888 in Paulding County, Georgia, James C. Moore was a Baptist minister, singing-school and public school teacher, and gospel composer. After attending Draketown Baptist Institute, the Berry Schools, and Mercer University, he studied music with his father, Charles R. Moore, L.Y. Allood, and B.B. Beall. His five hundred or more gospel songs have been published by nearly every gospel music publisher in America. *Where We'll Never Grow Old* has become a standard of gospel music.

James C. Moore   James C. Moore

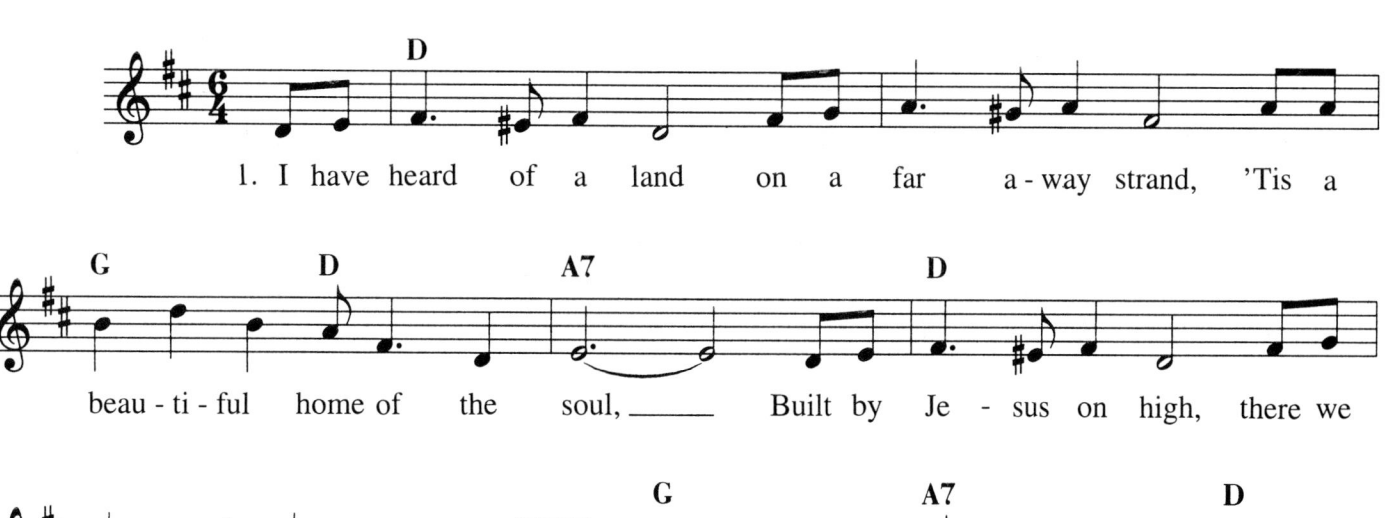

1. I have heard of a land on a far a-way strand, 'Tis a beau-ti-ful home of the soul, ___ Built by Je-sus on high, there we nev-er shall die, 'Tis a land where we nev-er grow old.

Chorus

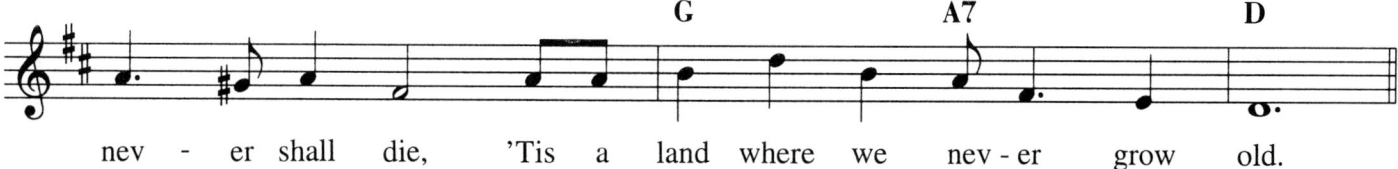

Bass: where we'll

Nev-er grow old, Nev-er grow old, In a land where we'll nev-er grow old,

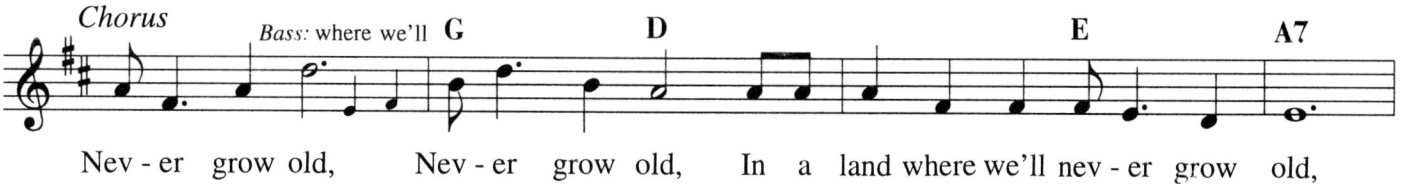

Bass: where we'll

Nev-er grow old, Nev-er grow old, In a land where we'll nev-er grow old.

2. In that beautiful home where we'll nevermore roam,
We shall be in the sweet by and by,
Happy praise to the King through eternity sing,
'Tis a land where we never shall die. *(Chorus)*

3. When our work here is done and the life-crown is won,
And our troubles and trials are o'er,
All our sorrow will end, and our voices will blend,
With the loved ones who've gone on before. *(Chorus)*

Will There Be Any Stars?

Eliza Edmunds Hewitt (1851-1920) was forty-six years old when she composed *Will There Be Any Stars?* A lifelong resident of Philadelphia, she taught both in the public schools and at Sunday school until a spinal sickness forced her to retire. While recuperating, she turned her talents to writing religious verse. Her poems were set to music by noted gospel composers such as William J. Kirkpatrick (*Lord, I'm Coming Home*) and John R. Sweney. It was Sweney who wrote the music to *Will There Be Any Stars?* A composer and bandleader during the Civil War, Sweney worked for over twenty-five years as a songleader at revivals.

E. E. Hewitt

John R. Sweney

1. I am thinking to-day of that beautiful land, I shall reach when the sun goeth down, When thro' wonderful grace by my Savior I stand, Will there be any stars in my crown?

Chorus

Will there be any stars, any stars in my crown, When at evening the sun goeth down? When I wake with the blessed in the mansions of rest, Will there be any stars in my crown?

2. In the strength of the Lord let me labor and pray,
   Let me watch as a winner of souls,
   That bright stars may be mine in the glorious day,
   When His praise like a sea billow rolls. *(Chorus)*

3. Oh, what joy it will be when His face I behold,
   Living gems at His feet to lay down,
   It would sweeten my bliss in the city of gold,
   Should there be any stars in my crown. *(Chorus)*

Wondrous Love

No one knows for certain who composed the lyrics or set the music to *Wondrous Love*. It is known that Silas M. Noel collected it as early as 1814. Some books such as the "Southern Harmony" and "Good Old Songs" attribute the authorship to J. Christopher, while the "Hesperian Harp" gives credit to Rev. Alex Means, from Oxford, Georgia.

2. When I was sinking down, sinking down, sinking down,
   When I was sinking down, sinking down,
   When I was sinking down, beneath God's righteous frown,
   Christ laid aside His crown for my soul, for my soul,
   Christ laid aside His crown for my soul.

3. To God and to the Lamb I will sing, I will sing,
   To God and to the Lamb I will sing,
   To God and to the Lamb, who is the great "I Am,"
   While millions join the theme, I will sing, I will sing,
   While millions join the theme, I will sing.

4. And when from death I'm free, I'll sing on, I'll sing on,
   And when from death I'm free, I'll sing on,
   And when from death I'm free, I'll sing and joyful be,
   And through eternity I'll sing on, I'll sing on,
   And through eternity I'll sing on.

Guitar Chords

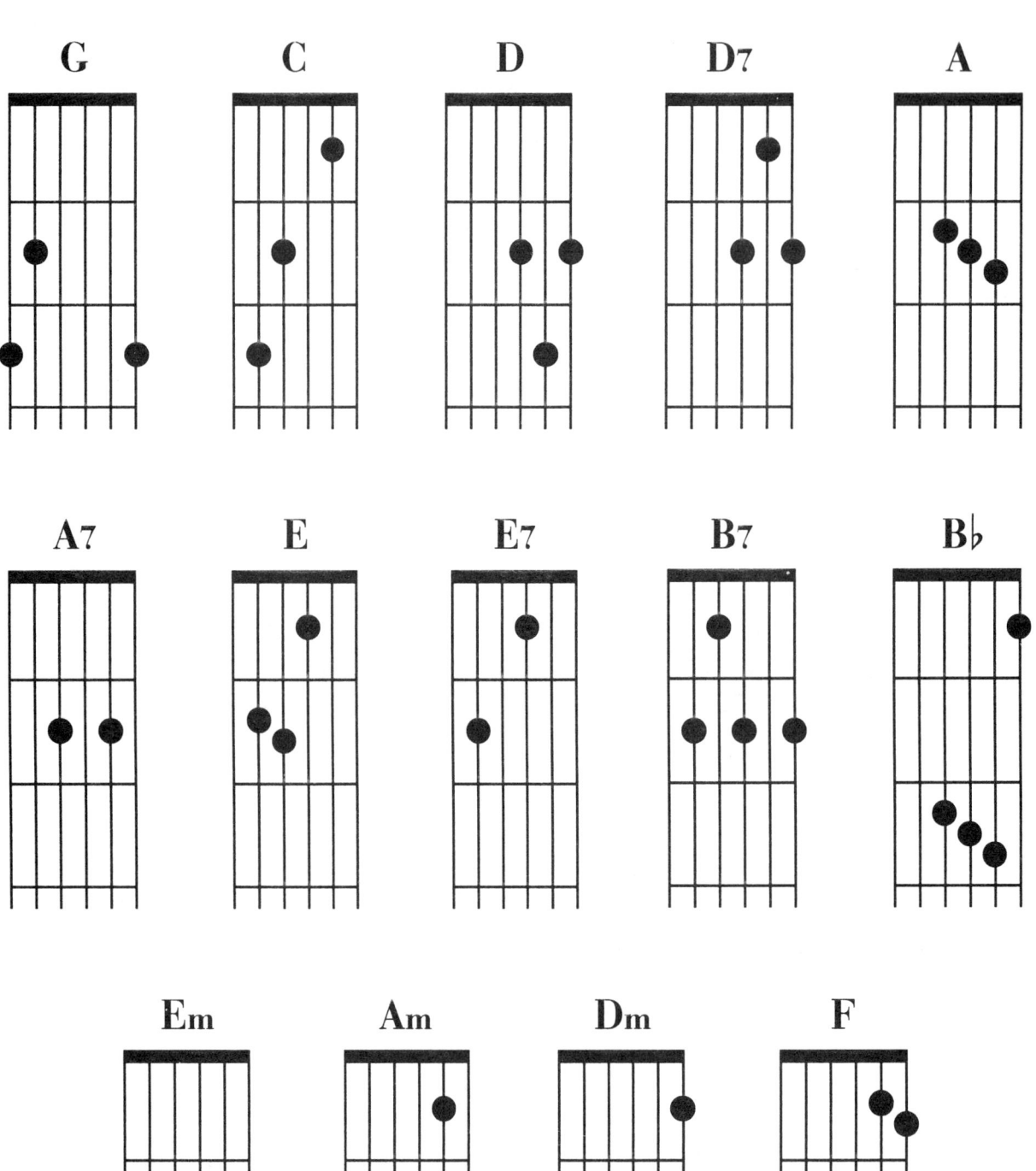

A Word of Thanks

Putting together a book on gospel music is akin to singing the lead part in a gospel quartet. Though the lead singer may pick out the material, set the tempo, and introduce the songs to the audience, he can't sing all the parts himself. In the course of the research for this book, many people willingly lent their voices, their ideas, and their old songbooks toward helping "The Old-Time Gospel Songbook" come together.

Thanks to Laura Boosinger for transcribing the music. My thanks also goes out to Barbara Swell, Janet Webb of PageScape Publications, Bob Willoughby, Hannah Jarvis, Walter Davis, Ray Greene, Betsey Farlow, Richard Dillingham, George Reynolds, Dick Terrior, Boyd Wright, The Historical Foundation in Montreat, North Carolina, Zeb Jolly, Quay Smathers, George Pullen Jackson, Stanley Bropson, Norm Cohen, Loretta Erbsen, David Holt, Loyal Jones, Berea College, Tina Liza Jones, Fred Park, The American Folklife Center, Mark V. Sanderford, Blanton Owen, Lyntha Eiler, Terry Eiler, Gerri Johnson, Carl Fleischhaer, Pat Mullen, John Vachon, Arthur Rothstein, John Delano, Dorthea Lange, Russell Lee, Roy Stryker, Marion Post Wolcott, Mary Jo Brezny, Marte Clark, Carol Elizabeth Jones, Stan Hancock, Ted White, Doug Swain, The North Carolina Division of Archives and History, and The Country Music Hall of Fame library.

Thanks to all!

Wayne Erbsen

Cedar Grove, North Carolina, May 1940
Photo by Jack Delano
Reproduced from the collections of the Library of Congress

Wayne Erbsen has been involved in early country and gospel music for some thirty years now. As a teacher, writer, recording artist, and performer, he has carried his music to all parts of the country and even Europe. Now residing in Western North Carolina with his wife and three children, Wayne is director of the Appalachian Music Program at Warren Wilson College in Swannanoa, North Carolina.

Wayne Erbsen
Photo by Wilson Somerville

Paynes Chapel in Sandy Mush, North Carolina, 1889
Photo by Mary Jo Brezny

Other Fine Books & Tapes

by

Wayne Erbsen

BOOKS

The Backpocket Bluegrass Songbook

The Backpocket Old Time Songbook

Bluegrass Banjo Simplified!

Clawhammer Banjo for the Complete Ignoramus!

The Complete & Painless Guide to the Guitar

Front Porch Old Time Songbook

Painless Mandolin Melodies

Starting Bluegrass Banjo From Scratch

• •

TAPES

Cold Frosty Morning

The Home Front

Front Porch Favorites

Native Ground

Old Time Gospel Instrumentals

Southern Mountain Classics

Southern Soldier Boy

Native Ground Music
109 Bell Road
Asheville, NC 28805
To Order Call 704-299-7031 or 1-800-752-2656